Information Technology—A Practical Course

Information Technology

A Practical Course

Harriet Harper

Senior Lecturer in Business Computing
North East Surrey College of Technology

MACMILLAN
EDUCATION

First published 1988

Published by
MACMILLAN EDUCATION LTD
Houndmills, Basingstoke, Hampshire RG21 2XS
and London
Companies and representatives
throughout the world

Typeset by P & R Typesetters Ltd, Farnham, Surrey

Printed in Hong Kong

British Library Cataloguing in Publication Data
Harper, Harriet
    Information Technology: a practical
    course.
    1. Information systems
    I. Title
    001.5

    ISBN 0–333–46086–3 tutor's book
    ISBN 0–333–46087–1 student's book

Contents

Acknowledgements

Special thanks to Andreas Credé. Thanks are also due to Sandra Lawrence, Nader Moghaddam, Julie Thorbes, Joyce Coope, Jean Spackman, The Information Technology Development Unit, Sandra MacBeth, and those students who worked through the assignments.

PART I
COMPUTERS AND WHAT
THEY CAN DO

1 Introduction to Computers

This book is concerned mainly with **microcomputers** (see figure 1) which are sometimes called **micros**, **desk-top computers, personal computers** or **PCs**. The practical assignments in Parts II and III are designed to be completed using this type of computer. However, before looking into microcomputers in more detail it is worth mentioning other types of computers, namely **mainframes** and **minis**.

Types of computer

The differences between mainframes, minis and micros—in terms of what they are used for—is becoming more blurred as micros become faster, more powerful and cheaper. There is, therefore, some degree of overlap. Today's desk-top micro is far more powerful than the very large mainframe computers of forty years ago. However, mainframes and minis still have to be used where micros are not robust, reliable or powerful enough.

Figure 1   A microcomputer (courtesy of Apple Computer UK Limited)

Mainframes

Mainframes are used when:

- Vast amounts of information need to be processed, often for 24 hours a day
- Reliability is essential. Mainframes are far less likely to break down ('crash') and if they do, alternative ways of processing the information in time are automatically made available
- It is essential that processing is completed within a certain time-limit, for example, for very large accounting systems (such as for local authorities), for social security payments or for weather forecasting. Information processed overnight is frequently needed by large organisations the following morning, for example, in currency dealing or foreign trading in large banks
- Where large numbers of users need access to a computer at the same time, such as for viewdata and information services

Minicomputers

The difference between mainframes and minis is mainly one of scale. Although minis are still more robust and powerful than micros, they are smaller, less powerful and cheaper than mainframes. They are used:

- In organisations where large amounts of information need to be processed, such as in large payroll systems
- Where a number of employees need access to the system at the same time and so use desk-top terminals which are linked to the mini
- In ships, aircraft or anywhere else where mainframes are too large to be accommodated

The computer system

Whatever type of computer you use it is always made up of the following (see figure 2):

- An **input** device, which allows you to 'put' information 'in' the computer. For micros, this is usually a keyboard and/or a mouse
- An **output** device, which displays the information coming 'out' of the computer. This is usually a screen and/or a printer
- The **processor,** or Central Processing Unit (CPU), which handles the input, processes it and then sends it to the output device. Housed inside the computer, in the form of one or more silicon chips, it is not visible to the user
- The **memory** is also in the form of chips and is where information is stored before, after and during processing. The amount that can be stored depends on the computer and determines its 'power'

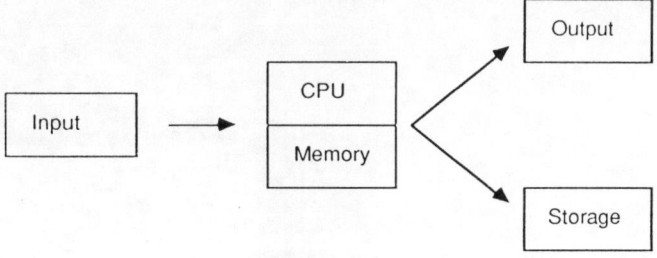

Figure 2

● A **storage** device to ensure that the information which has been input can be kept and accessed again. For micros, this is usually one or more disk drives for use with hard or floppy disks

Input devices

Types of input devices:

most common

keyboard

mouse

other types

touch screen

light pen

digitiser

optical character recognition

voice recognition

Keyboard   A keyboard is the most common input device. Users therefore have to have some keyboarding (typing) skills to use a computer efficiently.

Mouse   Many micros have a mouse as well as a keyboard. The mouse is a hand-held pointing device. When you move it around on a desk, the **cursor** (marker) on the screen moves in the same direction. By pointing with the mouse, 'dragging' it or clicking one or more of the 'buttons' on it, you can perform a range of activities.

Touch screen   The screen is divided into touch-sensitive areas, each displaying a choice of activities. To choose one of the activities, the user simply touches that section of the screen.

Light pen   Light transmitted from an instrument that looks like a pen can choose an activity or draw on the screen.

Digitiser   You can trace over a drawing with a digitiser and it will reproduce that drawing on the screen.

Figure 3   Keyboard and mouse (courtesy of Research Machines Limited)

Optical character recognition (OCR)   Certain sorts of typed documents on paper can be 'read' by an OCR device which can then transfer them directly to the computer.

Voice recognition   Some systems can respond to a limited number of spoken words.

Output devices

screen

printer

plotter

sound synthesizer

Screen   All micros use screens as an output device. The screen (**monitor** or **VDU**) can be **monochrome,** which means that it displays a single colour against a different colour background, or colour, which can display a variety of colours. For those systems which have a facility to create **windows**, the screen can be split into a number of sections so that you can view more than one document or activity at the same time.

Printers   transfer output on to paper. There is a range of different types of printer. The most common types are:

laser

dot matrix

daisy wheel

Laser printers produce professional-quality output. Text and graphics can be printed on the same page. Text can be in a range of **fonts** (typefaces and styles) and **point** sizes (size of characters). Laser printers produce a page at a time by using a fine beam of light (laser) scanning a drum coated with light-sensitive material. They are almost silent.

Dot matrix printers strike a pattern of closely spaced dots against a ribbon to form characters. The closer the dots, the better the quality. When the dots are very close together the quality of output can be **near letter quality** (NLQ). Dot matrix printers can be used for graphics and a range of fonts and point sizes but the quality is not as good as on a laser printer.

Daisy wheel printers use a circular wheel which strikes against an ink ribbon to create letter-quality characters. The wheel has a character on the tip of each 'petal'. Wheels can be changed for different typefaces but it is not really possible to have more than

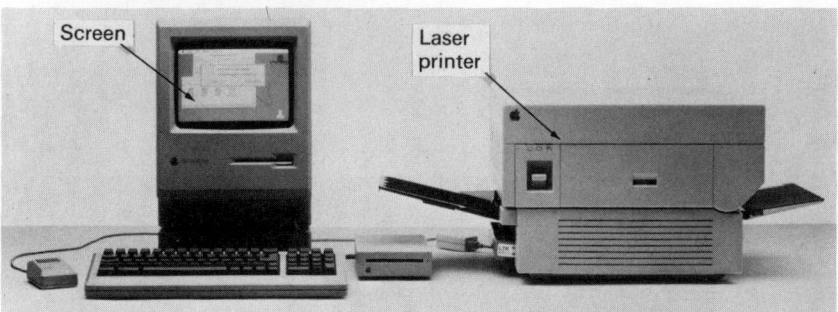

Figure 4   Laser printer (courtesy of Apple Computer UK Limited)

one typeface in a document. Daisy wheel printers are not suitable for graphics.

Plotters   also transfer output to paper and are used for colour graphics. Graphics and text can be drawn on a plotter by signals from the computer which guide a coloured pen across a piece of paper. Most plotters can automatically change pens.

Sound synthesizers can put sounds together to make words or music.

Storage

Information is usually stored on:

floppy disks

hard disks

optical disks

tapes

Floppy disks   There are two main types of floppy disks—$5\frac{1}{4}$ inches or $3\frac{1}{2}$ inches in size (8-inch disks are less common). The smallest type are the most durable because of their harder covering, and they often hold as much information as the larger ones. The type that you use depends on the disk drive on your computer. The

Figure 5   Three sizes of floppy disks (courtesy of Inmac (UK) Limited)

disks are split into 'sectors' which store separate sections of information. To create sectors which your type of computer can read, you have to **format** new disks before you use them for the first time. The disk drive can then **read** from that disk (find information) and **write** to it (record information on to the disk). The amount of data that floppy disks can store is measured in **kilobytes** (Kbs). One kilobyte is about one thousand characters.

Hard disks   Many micros now have one hard disk drive and one floppy disk drive next to it. The hard disk is in a sealed unit and is not visible to the user. Hard disks can store much more information than floppies and they are less prone to accidental misuse. When you buy an application program, such as a word processing package, it usually comes on several floppy disks. You can then transfer the programs on these disks to the hard disk; this saves you having to use several program disks every time you use that application. The amount of data that a hard disk can store is measured in **megabytes** (Mbs). One megabyte is about one million characters.

Optical disks   There is a range of different types of optical disk, the most common being **compact** disks or **CD-Roms**. They are read by laser and can store enormous amounts of data. Types available now can store at least 600 Mbs, which is equivalent to the output of someone typing 90 words a minute, 8 hours a day, 5 days a week for 8 years! Those that are 'read only' (which means that you can read from them, but you cannot store data on them) are not useful as storage systems but are excellent for very large, fixed databases. Those disks which are 'write once read mostly' (WORM) can be written to by a user but information cannot then be erased. These are useful where it is important to maintain permanent unchangeable records. Those which are 'read, write and erasable' are the most suitable for most users. Optical disks are removable and therefore transportable and saleable. The Post Office, for example, now sells all the country's 23 million addresses and postcodes on one compact disk.

Tapes   Cassette tapes are not usually used as main storage media in commerce or industry, but are still used by personal computer users. However, cassettes or reel-to-reel tapes are used to **back-up** (make copies of) data on hard disks on some systems.

Software

Hardware is the name given to the physical parts of a computer, for example, the screen, keyboard and printer.
Software refers to sets of instructions which control the computer and enable it to perform useful tasks. Without software, a computer is therefore useless.

There are two main types of software:

systems software (or operating systems)

application software

Systems software/operating systems   This type of software instructs the computer how to work. Just as the human brain co-ordinates the movements of different parts of the body, like arms and legs, the operating system controls the add-ons (**peripherals**) such as the disk drive or printer. Some of the better known operating systems are:

MS-DOS

PC-DOS

CP/M

UNIX

The operating system enables the user to install and use application software (software for a specific application, such as word processing or accounting). It also enables the user to perform **house-keeping** tasks such as formatting disks, listing, copying and deleting files, although many of these tasks can also be done in the application software. It may also include 'communications software' which enables computers to be linked to each other.

DOS (Disk Operating System) commands can be quite complex for an inexperienced computer user and there are, therefore, several types of software which act as a link between the user and the operating system. These programs, often referred to as **environments**, are usually very user-friendly and often make use of WIMPs, meaning windows, icons, mouse and pointers.

Application software

Application software or **packages** are designed to enable the user to perform specific tasks. The most popular types of packages are:

word processing

spreadsheets

databases

graphics

business accounting

Although these packages could be written especially for an organisation by a programmer, it is more usual to buy an 'off-the-shelf' package, particularly as there is such a wide choice available.

Application packages are designed to be used with specific

operating systems (without an operating system, they would not work). If a word processing package, for example, is designed to 'run on' (work with) MS-DOS, it can be used with any computer which has this particular operating system and uses the same size disks. When computers have the same operating system and can therefore use the same application software, they are said to be 'compatible'.

Application packages are discussed in detail in subsequent chapters.

Recap	Types of computers	mainframe
		mini
		micro
	Computer system	input
		output
		processor
		memory
		storage
	Input devices	keyboard
		mouse
		touch screen
		light pen
		digitiser
		OCR
		voice recognition
	Output devices	screen
		printers:
		laser
		dot matrix
		daisy wheel
		plotter
		sound synthesizer
	Storage	floppy disk
		hard disk
		optical disk
		tape
	Software	operating system
		application software

2 Word Processing

Word processing helps in the preparation and production of any kind of text, from memoranda and letters to reports and books.

Different packages vary in the facilities they offer but all word processing software enables the user to create, save, edit, recall and print text.

Main advantages of using word processing

- Text editing facilities such as overtyping, inserting, deleting or moving characters allow you to correct errors easily, without having to re-type whole sections or to apply unsightly correction materials to a printed document
- **Documents** or **files** can be edited, recalled and stored for future use
- Several copies can be printed out and the user can experiment with the final layout (for example, by changing the margins or line spacing) without having to re-type the document each time
- Standard letters or paragraphs, which are used regularly, can be saved and recalled when necessary
- Users can concentrate on what they are actually writing, and freely 'compose' at the screen without having to worry unduly about typing errors or layout, both of which can be amended at a later stage

The presentation of documents

Experimenting with the layout of a document is called **formatting** or **reformatting**. Word processing formatting facilities almost always include the ability to:

- Change margins and line spacing
- Justify the right margin. This means that the text finishes in what appears to be a straight line when printed out. Compare text with an unjustified (or ragged) right margin (figure 7) and the same text with a justified right margin (figure 8).
- Embolden text, making characters look darker and thicker. This is often used for headings to make them stand out
- Centre words across the page. This is also used for headings
- Use tabs in a range of ways. This might include those which, when typing in columns of figures, align decimal points

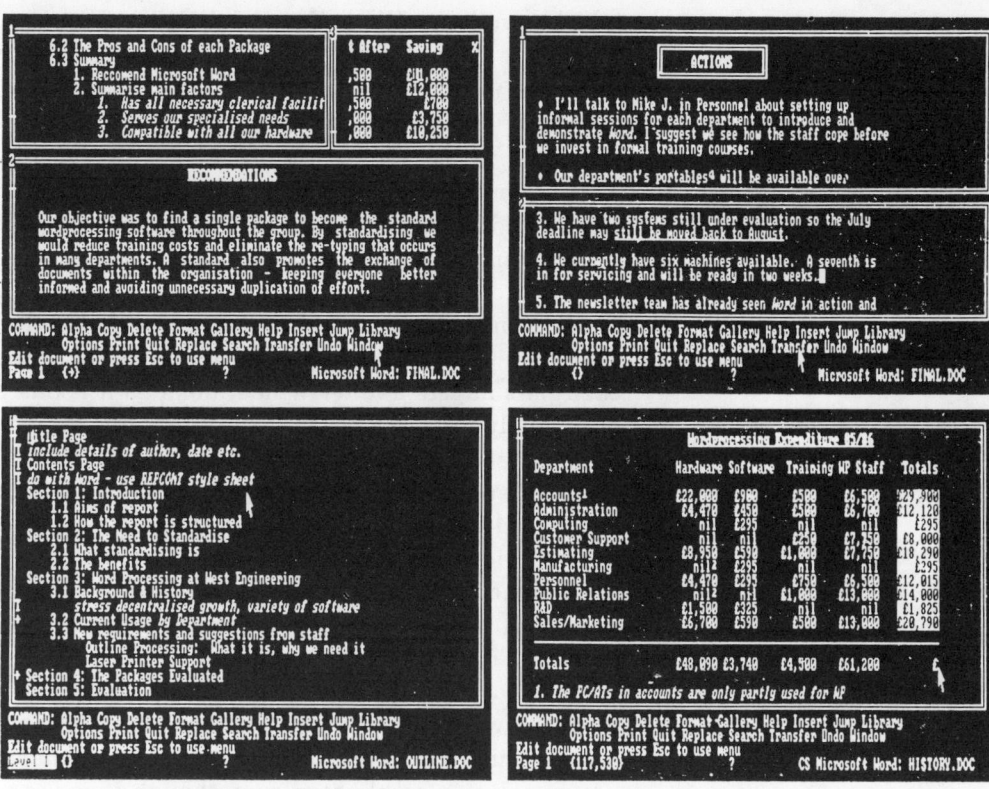

Figure 6 Word processing helps in the preparation and production of any kind of text (courtesy of Microsoft Limited)

```
Almost all word processing packages allow you
to format text so that the right margin is
justified.  This means that the last
character on each line finishes at the same
point across the page and the margin
therefore looks straight.
```

Figure 7

```
Almost all word processing packages allow you
to format text so that the right margin is
justified.    This    means    that    the    last
character on each line finishes at the  same
point  across  the  page  and  the  margin
therefore looks straight.
```

Figure 8

- Paginate, which means automatically divide a long document into pages of a specified length
- Automatically number pages

If the layout of a document on the screen is exactly how it will look when it is printed out, the type of system is called **WYSIWYG**, which stands for What You See Is What You Get. If a word is in italics, for example in a WYSIWYG system it will appear on the screen in italics.

Making text creation easier and better

The **mailmerge** facility makes it possible to produce 'personalised' letters and is available for most packages. Following the necessary instructions, one standard letter and a list of names and addresses can be brought together (**merged**) so that every time the letter is printed out it includes a different name and address from the list. The main body of the letter is only typed and proofread once, but each person gets a letter which looks as if it has been written specifically for him or her. A typical application would be a personalised 'mailshot' to a list of existing clients trying to sell them a new product. These types of mailshot could not possibly be performed manually to the same standard within a similar time period.

Spellcheckers, or dictionaries, are also designed to improve the quality of the final printed document (**hard copy**) by helping to eliminate spelling or typing mistakes. They are available for many word processing packages. Spellcheckers check words against words in their own dictionary and highlight them if a match cannot be found. This means, however, that names, towns and other proper nouns are also highlighted even though they are not necessarily misspelled. There is usually an option to add new words to the dictionary, so any proper nouns or technical terms which are frequently used can be added. Spellcheckers are good, therefore, for bringing to light typing errors and words which a user often misspells. They are also useful where the operator is unfamiliar with specific jargon. Many spellcheckers also include a thesaurus (listings of words that have similar meanings). It should be noted, though, that proofreading is still necessary as spellcheck programs are not 'intelligent'. They cannot, for example, distinguish between 'there' and 'their'.

Style-sheets are extremely useful if the same combinations of formats are used over and over again. Usually direct formatting, where you format a document as you create it, or using the **default** format (that is, the one that is already set and remains so unless the user changes it) is adequate for most purposes. However, as the range of formatting facilities increases and improves, thereby offering a very high standard of finished document, the user may be spending more and more time involved in this aspect of word processing and this can detract from the actual creation and typing of the text itself. Style-sheets, available on more sophisticated packages, are a very useful way to try to overcome this problem.

You may, for example, have a 'draft' style with double line spacing, wide margins and a large typeface for easy reading and editing, and then a 'final' style for how you want the final document to appear. This might be in three justified columns. Attaching a different style-sheet to a document before printing it does not involve any editing of the original document. Organisations can use style-sheets as a way of ensuring that everyone produces text with a consistent style. Setting up the style-sheets and learning how to use them may seem complex initially but, in the long term, time and frustration can be saved.

Another sophisticated facility is **outlining**, whereby the skeleton of a document, that is, just the main headings, is displayed. These headings can be unfolded to display other layers of headings or the text which lies behind a heading. This is useful when preparing or editing a long document with different layers of headings, sub-headings, sub-sub-headings and so on, where 'skipping through' the text on screen could otherwise be time-consuming and irritating.

Desk-top publishing

Anyone with a suitable microcomputer system on a 'desk top' can be a 'publisher'. Desk-top or electronic publishing, often referred to as DTP, extends the power of word processing to allow you to 'make-up' a page by mixing text (in a wide variety of type-face styles and sizes) with graphics. This means that you can create professional-looking newsletters, magazines, posters, invitations, letter-heads, logos, etc. DTP can also smarten up traditional documents like company reports, maintenance manuals, in-house training materials, sales and publicity literature and overhead transparencies.

DTP systems are usually very user-friendly and most make use of **mice, icons** and **pull-down menus** (see figure 9). Icons are small pictures on the screen which represent options or instructions. A clock, or hour glass, may appear on the screen, for example, to tell you to wait, or you may have to click the mouse on a drawing of a printer in order to print a document. Pull-down menus are lists of options which are 'pulled-down' like roller blinds from the top of the screen. The names of different type-styles, for example, are often listed in a pull-down menu.

Documents created in different packages—word processing, spreadsheet, database, business accounting or graphics—can be brought together on the screen and electronically **pasted-up** into a page. A whole range of sophisticated facilities exists to assist this process—sections can be enlarged, reduced, repositioned, copied and **cropped** to fit into a certain space. You can display the page in various sizes as well as **zoom in** to sections to make detailed viewing or editing easier.

To make full use of DTP software, it is necessary to have a high-quality printer (usually a laser printer). Dot matrix printers can

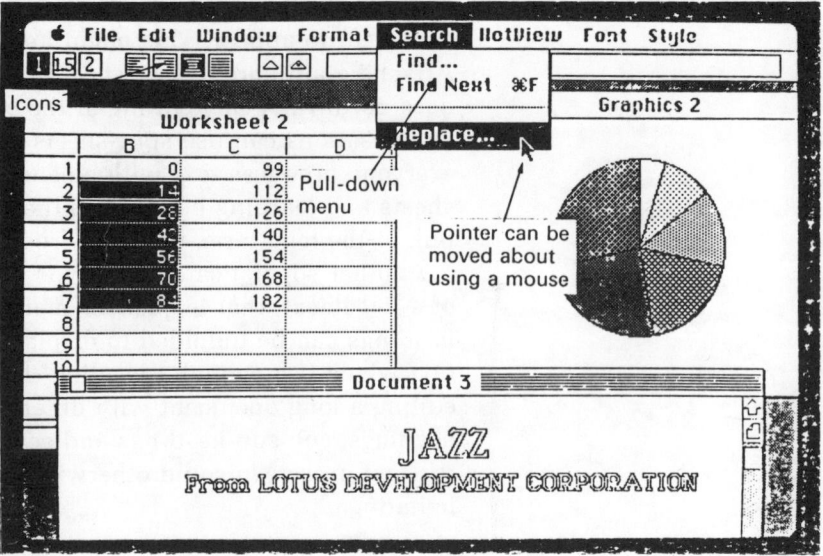

Figure 9 Using a mouse, icons and pull-down menus (courtesy of Lotus Development (UK) Limited)

Figure 10 With desk top publishing, text can be combined with graphics on the screen (courtesy of Apple Computer UK Limited)

also be used, although they cannot produce the same kind of professional print quality.

3   Spreadsheets

Spreadsheet packages are used in the preparation of a whole range
of business calculations. They are particularly suitable for
preparing budgets, financial forecasts and estimates.

A spreadsheet program produces an electronic 'piece of paper'
on the screen which is divided into a grid of small rectangles called
cells. These cells are identifed by numbers and letters so that the
cell in the top left-hand corner, for example, is usually referred to
as A1 or R1C1 (row 1, column 1).

When creating a spreadsheet (or **building a model**) you key in
headings, figures and formulae to make the calculations. The
example below shows how a garage works out its customers' bills.
It is a simple example but can be used to demonstrate the idea of a
spreadsheet.

	A	B	C	D	E
1				pounds	
2					
3	parts			65	
4	labour				
5		hourly	no. of		
6		rate	hours		
7					
8		9.00	2	18.00	
9					
10				———	
11					
12	total	without	VAT	83.00	
13	15% VAT			12.45	
14				———	
15	total	with	VAT	95.45	

In this model:

● Although 18.00 appears in cell D8, the user keyed in a formula
  meaning multiply B8 by C8 (usually typed as B8*C8). The
  computer stores the *formula* in that cell but prints out the result
  of the calculation on the screen. As long as the model remains

17

unchanged, the number in D8 will always be whatever is in B8 multiplied by whatever is in C8

Similarly:

- The formula for D12 is D3 plus D8 (usually typed as D3 + D8)
- The formula for D13 is 15 per cent of D12 (usually typed as 0.15*D12)
- The formula for D15 is D12 plus D13 (usually typed as D12 + D13)

The advantages of using a spreadsheet

If you were to change the hourly rate from £9.00 to £10.50, for example, you would edit cell B8; then the other cells which are affected by this change (D8, D12, D13, and D15) would automatically be updated.

Any figures can easily be amended and formulae can also be changed, if necessary. Rows and columns can be inserted, deleted, moved and copied. As spreadsheets are almost always larger than the size of the screen, you can only see one section of them at a time. However, you can move around a model speedily, either with the cursor (using a mouse or the cursor keys) or by referencing a particular cell with a GOTO or JUMP command; for example, GOTO M98 would take you directly to that cell.

There is a whole range of built-in functions for calculations which are frequently used. To add rows or columns, for example, you do not need to key in long formulae with lots of + signs.

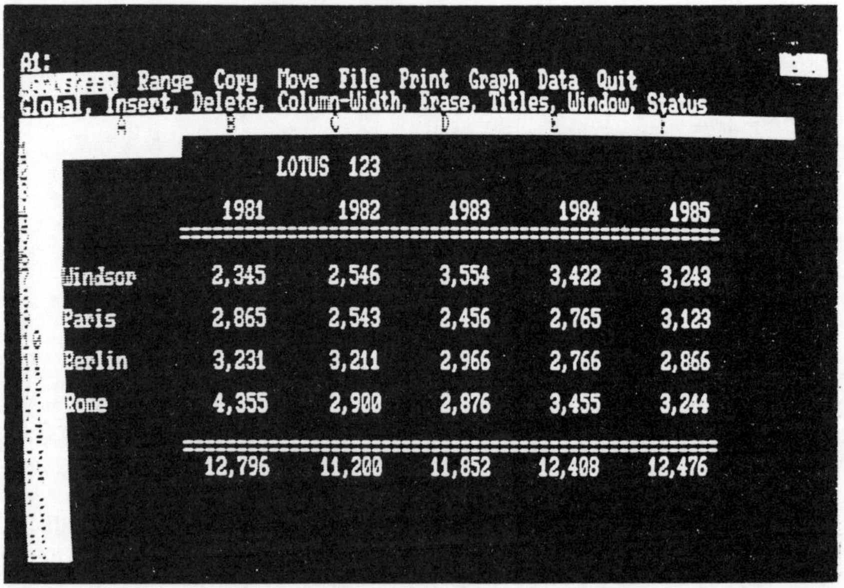

Figure 11   A spreadsheet model (courtesy of Lotus Development (UK) Limited)

Instead, you can use a particular command (usually SUM) and then identify the figures to be added, either by highlighting the relevant block with the mouse or by keying in the cell references of the first and last figures to be added. The method varies according to the package but the use of built-in functions, which is common to all packages, is a much easier and quicker way of creating formulae and, because less typing is involved, there is less chance of errors being made.

Another very useful, time-saving device is the copy (or **replicate**) facility. As well as copying rows and columns, formulae can also be copied. If, for example, you have four columns each of three figures, as below, and you want a total for each column, you can create the necessary formula for the total of the first column and then replicate it for the other three. The same formula will work for the other three columns because the computer stores that formula, *not* as 'add A2, A3 and A4', *but* as 'add up the figures in the three cells above this one'.

	A	B	C	D
1				
2	67	59	21	109
3	45	109	34	55
4	56	34	67	88
5	Total			

Other advantages of using a spreadsheet include the ability to save different versions without having to key in the whole model

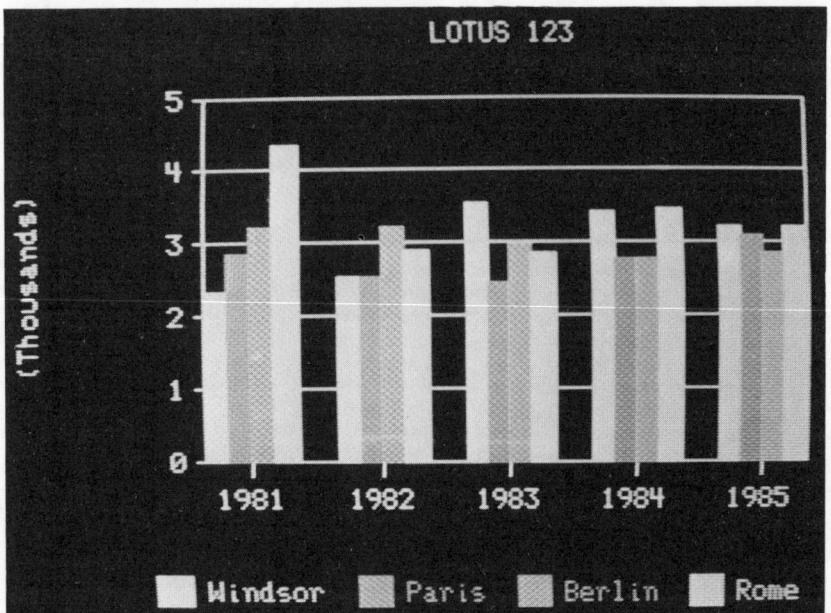

Figure 12 Some packages allow you to show spreadsheet models in graphical form (courtesy of Lotus Development (UK) Limited)

each time, and also the ability to print out one or more versions of a model. There is usually an option to include the actual formulae in print-outs.

Some packages allow you to show spreadsheet models in graphical form, and some also include database and word processing facilities.

What...if...?

Spreadsheets are most commonly used to answer so-called **what...if...?** questions. If, for example, you were starting up a small business you could build a spreadsheet model to prepare a business plan. This might include what you expect to earn and what your expenses will be. You could then 'play through' a range of options to see how various changes would affect your profit: what if your rent goes up?; what if you change the price of your product or service?; what if you spend more on advertising?; and so on. If you intend to show this model to your bank in order to get a loan, you may wish to play around with the figures until you get the profit figure that you know the bank will want to see.

---

4   Databases

Database application packages allow you to store information and
then find any part of that information quickly and without
difficulty. They are therefore primarily concerned with the storage
and retrieval of information in a way that can be determined by the
user. The application may vary from a simple system for keeping a
mailing list up-to-date, to a complex system for handling the
running of an entire business.

Because organisations keep and use information in different
ways, packages vary in their flexibility and in the specific features
they offer. However, certain ideas and terms are common to all
database packages.

Records

In creating a new database you start with an empty record, which
is like a blank card in a manual card index system (figure 13).

A BLANK RECORD

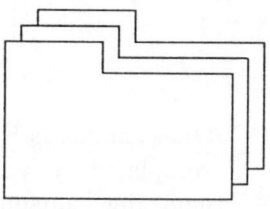

Figure 13

Fields

To put information into the record, you have to decide on the **fields**
you need. These fields are given **field names** (figure 14). For a
straightforward mailing list containing just names and addresses,
these field names are likely to be: NAME, ADDRESS, TEL. Care
should be taken at this stage in deciding exactly what fields you
need. If, for example, you later want a list of all the people in a
particular town or county, it would be better to subdivide
ADDRESS into fields such as STREET, TOWN, COUNTY and
POSTCODE. You might also want to divide NAME into FIRST,
SURNAME and TITLE in case you want to use the list for envelope
labels or want an alphabetical list of all surnames or even want to
search for all the Mr's.

21

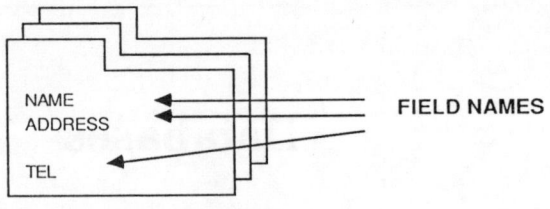

Figure 14

In establishing the fields, you may have to say which fields, when filled in, will contain characters (that is, letters) and which will contain numbers. Where you specify numbers, the computer will be able to perform mathematical calculations, if required. If there was a field called AGE, the user could then search, for example, for all those people with an AGE which is greater than 25. Some fields may contain numbers but are in fact 'characters' in that they will not be involved in any kind of calculations. Typical examples are telephone numbers.

A COMPLETED RECORD

Figure 15

Files

Once the fields have been established, the records are ready to be completed by typing in the relevant information. This aspect is the most time-consuming part of creating a database. A series of records which have the same format (design) is called a **file** (see figure 16) and each file is give a file name, for example LIST1.

A FILE CONTAINING A

NUMBER OF RECORDS

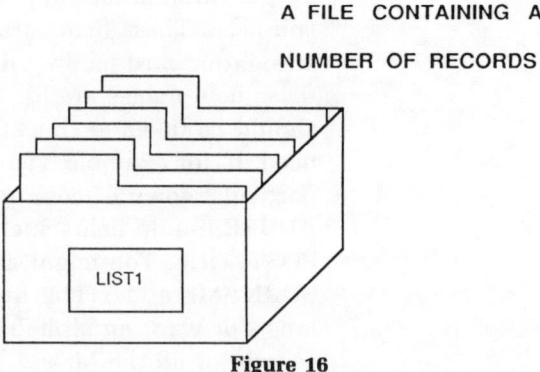

Figure 16

Within the file, data held in the various fields can be updated and amended as and when necessary. This may involve completing a new record for a new client, deleting a record, or simply amending details on existing records such as a change of address. Amending the fields themselves, once all the data has been entered, is more complex and that is why it is important to think carefully about the fields when creating them initially.

Some packages offer password facilities. Personnel records on a database file, for example, would contain salary details and a password, known only to authorised users, could stop other people who know how to use the package from looking at that particular file.

Using the database file to find information

To search for information you can **query** a database (this means ask questions). To search through all the records in a file for those clients who live in Harlow, for example, the **keyfield** would be TOWN. Different packages have different ways of asking the questions, but it is likely to be something like FIND TOWN = "HARLOW".

You can also search for information using more than one **criteria**. To query the database for all those clients who live in Harlow and are over 30, the question might look like FIND TOWN = "HARLOW" AND AGE > 30. The number of criteria you can use in one search depends on the package. Another method of extracting information is to search for **character strings** (that means a certain group of letters). This is usually slower than keyfield or criteria searches. To find information on reptiles, for example, in a database giving details of books and journals, a search could be made through all the records to extract those where the word 'reptile' appears.

Generating reports

As well as extracting information, most databases can also combine it into a report. This is called **report generation**. This may just be a list of names and addresses, which is useful for repetitive mailing lists, or may involve elaborately designed forms with information extracted from a number of files.

If a package is **multi-file**, as opposed to **single-file**, more than one file can be accessed at once and links may be set up between records.

Programmable databases

With a **programmable** database package, certain processes which occur frequently can be completed automatically, by writing a **program**. Learning how to do this is like learning computer programming and so this type of software is likely to be more complex to use. While non-programmable packages are concerned

```
SCH     :123
HOUSE   :[BOUNDS GREEN]
FORENAME:WILLIAM
SURNAME :NUTTING
REL     :H
HSZ     :3
FSZ     :3
CON     :M
SEX     :M
AGE     :23
OCCUP   :FARM LABOURER
OCODE   :10101
TBIRTH  :DATCHWORTH
CBIRTH  :HERTS
CCODE   :HRT
REMARKS :
YEAR    :1881
--------------------------------------------------------------------
SCH     :123
HOUSE   :[BOUNDS GREEN]
FORENAME:ALICE
SURNAME :NUTTING
REL     :W
HSZ     :3
FSZ     :3
CON     :M
SEX     :F
AGE     :25
OCCUP   :
OCODE   :99999
TBIRTH  :WELWYN
CBIRTH  :HERTS
CCODE   :HRT
REMARKS :
YEAR    :1881
--------------------------------------------------------------------
SCH     :123
HOUSE   :[BOUNDS GREEN]
FORENAME:CHARLES
SURNAME :NUTTING
REL     :S
HSZ     :3
FSZ     :3
CON     :
SEX     :M
AGE     :0
OCCUP   :
OCODE   :99999
TBIRTH  :DATCHWORTH
CBIRTH  :HERTS
CCODE   :HRT
REMARKS :8 MONTHS
YEAR    :1881
--------------------------------------------------------------------

        627 records searched
          3 records matched
```

Figure 17   A print-out of a search (courtesy of The Advisory Unit)

with information storage and retrieval, programmable databases can also process transactions. In fact, many accounting packages are built on this type of structure.

You may, for example, have three database files: 'Customers', 'Products' and 'Materials' in a multi-file, programmable database. If so, you could program the computer to extract the customer's details from 'Customers' every time he or she placed an order, check the credit limit and, if it was satisfactory, extract the name and address and enter it automatically on to an invoice that you have designed. The computer would then check the appropriate record in the 'Products' file for the cost per item, and bill the invoice to the correct amount before it was printed out. The 'materials' file would then be automatically updated so that enough components were ordered to replace the depleted stock of manufactured products.

5 Graphics

Graphics refers to the ability to present computer output in the form of drawings, pictures or diagrams.

Two different types of graphics software will be discussed here: firstly, packages which allow the user to 'paint' or 'draw' shapes and symbols; and secondly, packages which produce graphical representations of numerical data (referred to as **business graphics**). These two applications may be combined in some packages.

Paint packages

Paint packages enable you to create a range of drawings—for example, posters, publicity material, logos or designs.

Most paint packages display a drawing area on the screen with a **toolbox** on one border and a **palette** of different colours and types of shading on another. Using a mouse (which for this kind of graphics software is almost a necessity), you select the tool you want to use from the toolbox and then the colour or shading you want from the palette.

If, for example, you want to 'paint' something on the screen in dark blue, you move the mouse to the icon (picture) of the paintbrush in the toolbox and then click the mouse. You then move the mouse to the dark blue area in the palette and click it again. Then, as you move the mouse about on your desk, a pointer moves across the screen producing a dark blue stream of 'paint'.

A range of other facilities—varying in sophistication—is usually available. As well as creating all sorts of shapes and moving them around the screen, you can duplicate sections automatically, cut out shapes and paste them in somewhere else on the screen, or **zoom in** to look at or edit a small part of a drawing and **zoom out** again. Foreground and background colours can be changed or inverted, shapes can be rotated or **flipped over**, and diagrams can be enlarged or reduced.

The toolbox usually contains an option for text (writing) so that text and graphics can be incorporated into the same document. Once the mouse has been clicked on the appropriate icon (usually a T), the keyboard can be used in the usual way to create text on the screen. Within this option, most packages offer a choice of fonts (text style) and point sizes (size/height of characters). The quality of the printed output will, of course, depend as much on the printer or plotter as on the software package.

Although there are similarities, the kind of paint package described above should not be confused with **computer-aided design** (CAD) software. CAD is used for technical drawings in areas such as engineering, electronics, architecture and interior design. CAD packages therefore need to be more sophisticated and flexible than straightforward 'paint' packages, particularly in their ability to scale and proportion the elements of a drawing.

Business graphics

These packages tend to be used mainly to produce graphs and charts for inclusion in business reports. In making facts, figures and trends more easily intelligible, the use of graphics can greatly enhance communication and presentation. The graphical representation of numerical data can be displayed directly on a screen or sent to a printer or plotter. Output can also be to overhead transparencies or slides, which can be used as visual aids when giving a presentation.

Business graphics packages can be bought as **stand-alones** or can be part of **integrated** packages. Integrated packages usually include spreadsheet, database and word processing facilities as well as graphics. Many of the stand-alone packages, however, are designed so that they can, in fact, be integrated with other packages. The advantage of integration is the ability to create graphs and charts from data in existing spreadsheet worksheets or database records without having to key in the data more than once. Another advantage is the ability to electronically **paste** graphs into the middle of a document which contains mostly text. This is most effectively achieved, though, with graphics packages which can be incorporated into desk-top publishing programs.

Almost all business graphics packages enable you to produce pie, line and bar graphs. Pie charts are particularly suitable to demonstrate percentage shares (that is, how a whole 'cake' is divided up) but they are limited to one data range. This means you cannot use one pie chart to compare two or more sets of data. Line graphs are often used when a lot of numbers or details are needed. They can very effectively show trends such as the rate of inflation, sales figures or profits over several months or years. More than one line graph can be displayed at a time. Bar charts or histograms are very versatile business graphics tools. The bars can be shown vertically or horizontally and, using different colours or types of shading, several data ranges can be displayed either as individual bars or as segments of one bar.

The more sophisticated the package, the more refinements there are to these basic types of graphs. Dramatic effects can be achieved, for example, by the use of three-dimensional graphics. Many packages also include facilities to produce other types of graphs such as scatter graphs, organisational charts and bubble

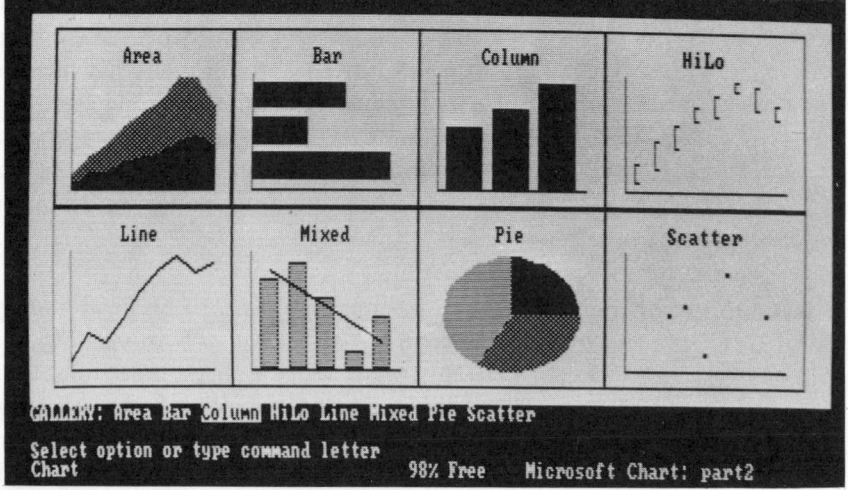

Figure 18   This package offers eight types of graph (courtesy of Microsoft Limited)

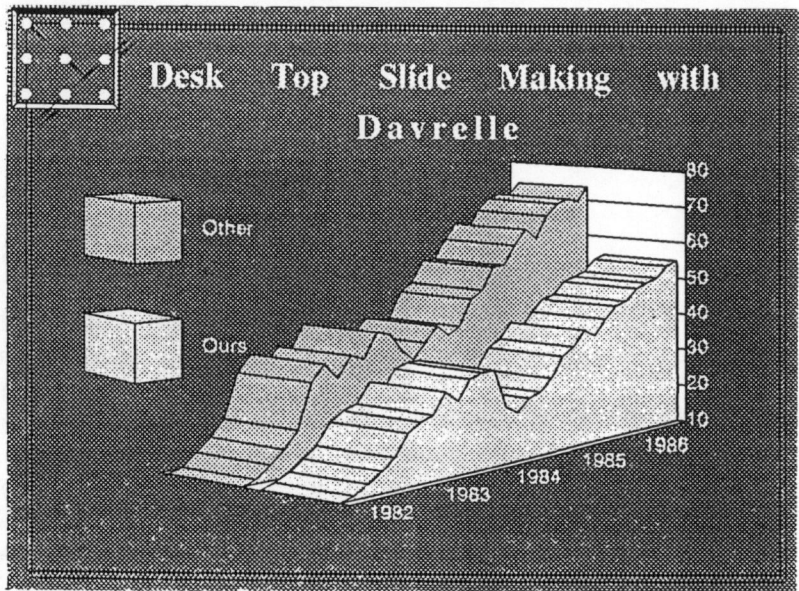

Figure 19   Three-dimensional graphics (courtesy of Soft Image Systems)

charts. One very effective presentation technique involves the use of pre-designed symbols (some packages also allow you to design your own). In this way you could, for example, display election results as lines of different coloured matchstick humans, or export statistics as a line of crates.

The most flexible packages enable the user to change any of the elements of the graph or chart, once it is created, and add or edit text, symbols and diagrams.

6   Videotex

Videotex is a means of displaying screen-sized pages (or frames) of information, usually in the form of pictures (graphics) and writing (text), on a TV or computer screen.

There are two main types of videotex—viewdata and teletext. With teletext the information is broadcast over the air and so it is a one-way system. Viewdata, on the other hand, is a two-way or interactive communication system. This means that with viewdata systems, messages and requests can be sent *and* received.

Teletext

Teletext is broadcast on TV channels at the same time as other TV programmes. BBC and ITV have their own teletext systems— Ceefax and Oracle respectively. With a special teletext adaptor (often already fitted to television sets) and a remote control teletext keypad, the pages can be accessed via menus.

Figure 20   A Ceefax page (courtesy of the British Broadcasting Corporation)

The pages are broadcast one after another as a continuous stream and once broadcast, the cycle starts again. The cycle stops at the number of the page you have keyed in and if that number happens to be near the end of the cycle you will have to wait for a minute or so before it appears on the screen. It is not possible to skip the beginning of the cycle and go directly to the page you want.

Teletext provides news, weather reports, sports results, details of TV programmes, subtitles for the hard of hearing, information on travel and finance, recipes, games and a lot more.

Viewdata

Viewdata by phone

Using telephone lines to link you to a central computer, you can not only call up information but also respond to it. You can therefore use viewdata systems for electronic mail (leaving and receiving messages), teleshopping, telebanking and telebooking.

Figure 21   Teleshopping from home (courtesy of British Telecom)

As well as a television set and keypad, or a computer with the necessary software, you need a modem. A **modem** (short for **mo**dulator/**dem**odulator) is a device which converts computer data into signals that can be sent over the phone and back again.

How do you use viewdata?

To use such a viewdata system, you telephone the viewdata computer and it answers your call by displaying information on the screen and asking you for your user number and password. (These are given to you when you register as a subscriber. You usually have to pay for this as well as paying for the phone calls.) Having logged on to the computer, you can then use the electronic mail, if available, or call up pages from a series of menus or indexes. As well as finding the pages you want from the relevant database and sending them to you, the central computer will also be dealing with all the other viewdata users at the same time.

Who provides the information?

Prestel, one of the most widely used viewdata systems, is provided by British Telecom. There are also a number of other viewdata services, some specialising in specific areas of information such as finance, medicine or law. However, while viewdata services provide the computing power, they do not usually provide all the database information themselves. **Information providers** (IPs), like banks, airlines, businesses, newspapers and government agencies, send (usually electronically) their own information to the viewdata computer and are responsible for updating it.

Closed user groups (CUGs)

IPs may wish to restrict access to their information, in which case an additional password is required. Access is then refused to users who do not know the password. This facility is useful as a communication service for the employees of organisations with branches in different locations. Many travel agency chains use CUGs in this way. Sales companies, too, find the service extremely useful as orders can easily be transmitted to an office from a sales force or from retailers and wholesalers. In some cases, anyone can join a closed user group for a fee or form an individual group. Computer hobbyist groups, for example, use viewdata services for advertisements, letters, news, reviews, etc. and also to transmit (or **download**) computer programs to their own computer.

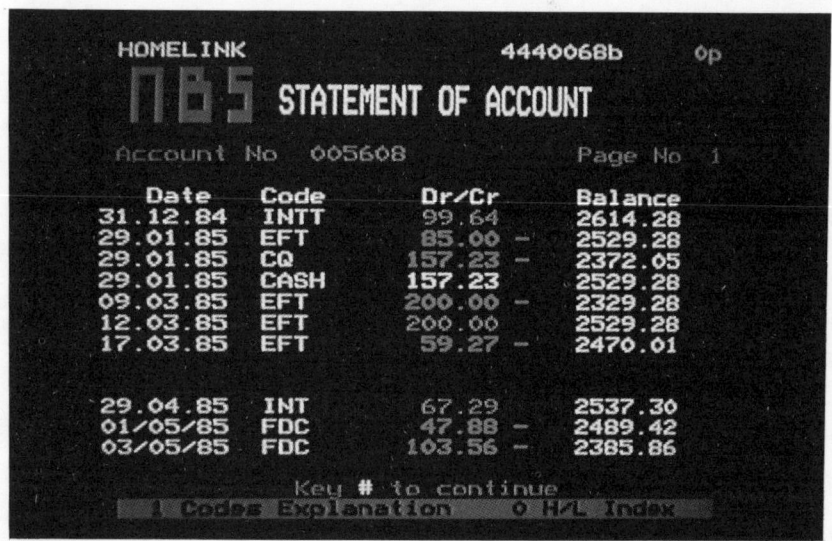

Figure 22 Telebanking with Prestel (courtesty of British Telecom)

Gateways

Many organisations have their own vast databases. When these are
linked to a viewdata system so that subscribers have direct access
to them, the link is called a **gateway**. With telebanking, for
example, access to a bank's computer usually enables you to look
up your account or make payments. Similarly, a viewdata gateway
to an airline database might allow you to look at arrival and
departure times and also make bookings.

Local viewdata systems

Viewdata systems can also be used without a telephone. With the
appropriate software, information can be received and sent to the
users of a local computer network. This is useful within
organisations for in-house electronic mail, electronic newsletters
and information on sales figures, prices, customer lists, etc.

With local viewdata systems you can create your own frames. As
well as being able to produce text, other facilities are usually
available. These vary, but are likely to include graphics, so that
pictures and diagrams can be designed, a choice of background or
foreground colours, and also double-height or flashing characters.
Pages need to be numbered and **routed** so that users can easily
access the required information. Routeing involves establishing a
series of menus, starting with one main menu and then branching
out to various sub-menus. Once created, pages can be edited, re-
routed, saved and printed. Printing can also include details of how
the pages are routed.

7   **Business Accounting**

'Business accounting' or 'business' computing packages cover a whole range of applications used in businesses and vary enormously in power, capability and cost.

In this chapter, the following applications will be discussed individually:

● Sales ledger

● Purchase ledger

● Nominal ledger

● Stock control

● Payroll

It should be noted, however, that different names may be used for programs that perform similar functions to those listed above. One program may, for example, be referred to simply as a **book-keeping** or **accounting** package. Many such programs are **integrated** which means that they combine more than one of the above applications. There are advantages to having integrated packages, as opposed to **stand-alone** (individual) ones.

A stand-alone sales ledger package, for example, may be all that a company needs. It is therefore likely to be cheaper and less complex than an integrated package. However, outputs of one application in business computing are often inputs to another. Invoice totals from sales invoicing, for example, are inputs to sales ledger and so it therefore makes sense to link these two programs. A fully integrated system, incorporating several applications, allows automatic transfer of data from one application to another without the need to key in the same information more than once.

Sales ledger

Where companies sell goods or services, they need to record information about their customers.

The main benefit of a sales ledger program is the ability to display on the screen information about any particular customer.

In a sales ledger program, details are kept on each customer. Details vary according to the program but are likely to include the account number, name and address, credit limit, balance brought forward and the transactions **posted to** (entered into) the account.

Updating the information involves posting new transactions as well as amending any of the standard information, such as changing an address or deleting or inserting new accounts.

As with other business computing packages, one of the main advantages of using a computer is the speed with which it can select and sort the information to produce printed **reports**. The nature of the reports varies but may include:

● A day book, listing all the transactions

● A debtors' list, showing those who have exceeded their credit limit

● Printed customer lists or labels (complete or selective)

● VAT reports

Sales ledger programs may or may not include sales invoicing (the two areas are obviously linked). For the production of invoices, two files are needed—a customer file and a product file. The product file contains a record of each type of product sold by the company, usually in the form of a product code, product description and price. A full invoice can be built up on screen, ready to be stored and printed out, often by just keying-in customer codes and product codes. The degree of complexity, however, varies according to the program, the document design and factors concerning the goods such as units of sale, pricing methods, discounts, etc.

Purchase ledger

Purchase ledger is similar to sales ledger. Instead of a customer file there is a supplier file. Updating, as with the sales ledger, involves posting transactions and amending standard information.

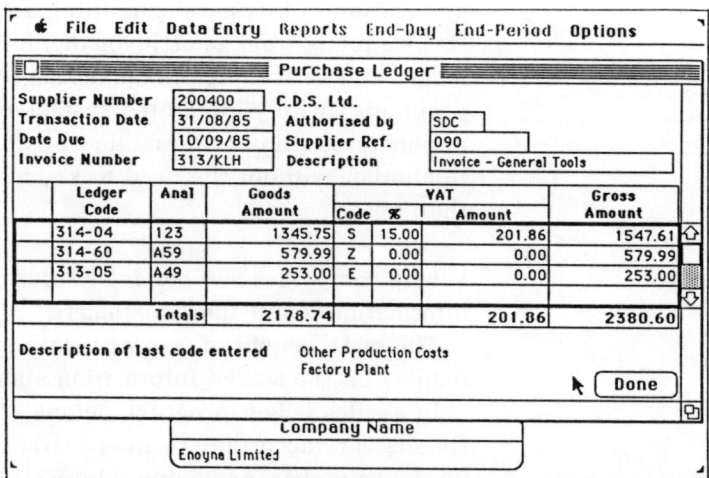

Figure 23   A purchase ledger file (courtesy of Apple Computer UK Limited)

The main benefit of purchase ledger programs is the ability to keep a strict control over payments and thereby make the best of the company's cash resources.

There is a range of options offered by most packages to allow for flexibility as to *how* and *when* suppliers are paid. Some companies, for example, prefer payment dates to be determined by the computer, based on standing rules and information held for each supplier; others prefer an operator to check through a computer-produced list of payments due.

Like the sales ledger programs, reports can be produced and these are likely to include, among other things:

● A day book, listing all invoices posted, and

● Remittance advices with cheques or credit transfers

Nominal ledger

The nominal ledger analyses income and expenditure, and in so doing provides an accounting summary of all the company's activities, assets and liabilities.

The main benefit of having a computerised nominal ledger is the ease and frequency with which the overall financial state of the business can be ascertained.

In the nominal ledger an account is opened for each source of income (for example, sales) and each type of purchase (for example, raw material), either for the whole organisation or for each department or section. As each transaction is posted to the relevant account, a new balance is calculated. With packages which allow for integration of sales, purchase and nominal ledgers, postings to the first two ledgers contain the appropriate nominal ledger account number so that details are automatically entered into the nominal ledger.

The calculation and cumulative totalling of VAT, as well as its breakdown into various sub-totals, is handled automatically.

Reports, as with the other ledgers, vary according to the package but are likely to include:

● Trial balance, providing an overall view of the state of the business, showing that debits and credits are in balance and giving totals for each account for a certain period

● Transactions list—daily lists or complete lists for audit purposes

● Lists showing expenditure or income, by type, and variances, if any, from budgets

● VAT reports

Stock control

Most packages offer a wide choice of facilities to accommodate the very different needs that businesses have in relation to stock control.

The main benefits for most businesses of a computerised stock control system are:

● The ease and speed with which one can find out the stock situation at any one time without the need to physically check it

● The ability to indicate usage, delivery lead times and the need to re-order

● The maintenance of an accounting record to ascertain stock values, which can help to minimise the capital tied up in stock

The key element of a stock control program is the stock file, which contains a record for every stock item. It is likely to include a number or code, description, actual stock level, re-order quantity, cost price and, depending on the package and the products, also retail price, suppliers' details and quantity on order.

Daily updating in respect of receipts, issues and returns to stock is essential.

Reports typically include:

● Complete or selective lists of stock items

● Orders printed, where new stock is needed according to the rules given in the program

● Activity report for audit purposes and also to assess whether or not order levels should be changed

Payroll

Payroll programs hold records for every employee.

The main benefit of a payroll program is the saving of clerical

| Bonus! v5.1 | | Edit Employee's Details | | | | (C) Intex 1987 | |

No 1	Employee Name	Dunston Arnold			N.I. Number	ZZ 55 54 54 B
Tax Code	364 L	Department	ADMIN		N.I. Rate	A	Week / Mth 1 ?	n
Payment Method	c	Bank Name				Payment Period	w
Cash Press [C] Cheque Press [Q] Bank Giro Press [B]		Bank Branch				Monthly = [M] Weekly = [W] 4 Weekly = [4]
		Account No		Code	- -	
Normal Hours	40.00	Bonus	0.00	Previous Tax	0.00
Salary	0.00	Company Sick P	0.00	Previous Gross	0.00
Rate of Pay	3.6700	Pension	- 80.00	Holiday Accrual	
Holiday Hours	160.00	Savings Fund	0.00	Holiday Rate	3.6700
Born	04.05.54	Started		Next Pay Tax No	9	Director n	Sex male

Figure 24   Payroll programs hold records for every employee (courtesy of Intex Software)

time that results from automatic calculations and the automatic repetition of unchanged data from one month to another.

Each employee's record usually contains information such as an employee number, name, tax code, standing deductions from pay, gross pay to date and tax to date. It will also have the annual salary, hourly rate, overtime rates or shift allowances, as is appropriate.

For employees with no change of circumstances since the last payment, as is the case for most salaried staff, no updating is required each month. Any changes, however, have to be keyed in and checked. Hours for hourly-paid staff, for example, may need to be updated every week or month.

Gross pay, National Insurance contributions, tax and net pay are all then automatically computed. P60 forms and Inland Revenue returns can also be printed at the end of the tax year.

Reports will certainly include the individual pay slips but may also include a list of bank credits.

PART II
PRACTICAL ASSIGNMENTS

8 Word Processing Assignments

By completing the word processing assignments, students will demonstrate the ability to:

1   LOAD a word processing program
2   LOAD a word processing document
3   CREATE a new document
4   ENTER text
5   INSERT text
6   DELETE text
7   REPLACE text
8   CHANGE margins
9   CHANGE line spacing
10 CENTRE text
11 EMBOLDEN text
12 UNDERLINE text
13 JUSTIFY margins
14 ALLOCATE vertical space from given measurements
15 PRESENT effective display of text using tabs
16 PAGINATE a multi-page document
17 NUMBER a multi-page document
18 COMPOSE a standard letter
19 MERGE two documents or INSERT variables into a standard letter
20 SAVE a document
21 PRINT a document
22 PRINT multiple copies of a document
23 EXIT from a word processing program

Objectives covered by each assignment

Assignment 1
(1), 3, 4, (5), (6), (7), 20, 21, (23)

Assignment 2
(1), 2, 5, 6, 7, 20, 21, (23)

Assignment 3
(1), 3, 4, 8, 20, 21, (23)

Assignment 4
(1), 2, 4, 8, 10, 21, (23)

Assignment 5
(1), 3, 12, 13, 20, 22, (23)

41

Assignment 6
(1), 3, 4, 11, 20, 21, (23)

Assignment 7
(1), 2, 4, 9, 11, 13, 16, 17, 20, 21, (23)

Assignment 8
(1), 2, 14, 16, 17, 21, (23)

Assignment 9
(1), 3, 4, (10), (11), (12), 15, 22, (23)

Assignment 10
(1), 3, 4, 5, 18, 19, 20, 22, (23)

Assignment 1

(a)   Create a new document with a suitable name and key in the text about 'Coriander' (use appropriate margins).
(b)   Proofread the text carefully and correct any errors.
(c)   Save the document.
(d)   Print out one copy.

CORIANDER

A culinary herb, coriander, is one of the ingredients of curry powder and hence found in many Indian recipes. The seeds are spicy, profusely produced by the plant, and combine well with cumin and other spices to produce the flavours in much Middle-Eastern and South-east Asian food.

Coriander seed is sown outdoors in sun and a light, well-drained soil in April-May, and thinned to about 20 cm apart. It grows quickly to about 60 cm tall and flowers profusely.

Assignment 2

(a)   The draft copy of the text about coriander (created in the previous assignment) needs editing. Recall the document and make the amendments listed below:

(i)   In the second sentence insert 'distinctively' before 'spicy' so that it reads: 'The seeds are distinctively spicy,...'.

(ii)   In the second paragraph, insert the word 'in' before 'a light) so that it reads:'...in sun and in a light, well-drained soil...'.

(iii) Replace 'April–May' with 'April/May'.

(iv) After '20 cm' insert '(8 ins)' and after '60 cm' insert '(2 ft)'.

(v) Delete the word 'quickly' in the last sentence.

(b) Reformat text if necessary.

(c) Save text and print out a copy which incorporates the above amendments.

Assignment 3

(a) Create a new document and key in the article about Leningrad.

(b) Save the document.

(c) Print out one copy.

LENINGRAD

One inch margin →

Most guidebooks describe Leningrad — quite rightly — as one of the world's most beautiful cities. Built on dozens of islands, it is often called the 'Venice of the North'. Visitors are struck by the soft shimmer of the canals with their poetic and colourful bridges and by the expanse of the city's main river, the Neva.

← one inch margin →

Taking holiday snaps is not easy — the city's sweeping squares and monumental buildings are too expansive for even the widest-angle lens. Monuments and palaces, painted avocado green, sky blue or pink, have been meticulously preserved. One can stand for hours admiring the architectural masterpieces, the church spires, domes and cupolas and the long broad avenues.

, yellow

In winter, the city looks its most romantic, buried under snow, although it can be extremely cold. In summer, when most tourists come to admire its beauty, Leningrad enjoys endless daylight, known as the 'White Nights'. Whatever the time of year, few people can resist the charm and elegance of Leningrad.

hoary

new para.

Assignment 4

(a) Recall the document about Leningrad.

(b) To make the layout of the text suitable for binding, the margins need changing. Make the left margin three cm and the right margin one and a half cm.

(c) Centre the heading.

(d) Print out an amended copy.

Assignment 5

(a)   The letter to Mr Sargent is from Roof-Rooms Inc., 23 Barnes Place, Cardiff, Wales.

(b)   Key in the letter.

(c)   Save the document.

(d)   Print out two copies—one to send and one for the file.

(e)   Sign the one to send, on behalf of John Pickering.

Mr Sargent
25 Acre Lane
Swansea   Date today
W. Glamorgan

Dear Mr S

Loft conversion

Thank you/ for your letter of (last Monday – check date).] Justify right margin for whole letter
In response to your questions:

1. I confirm that I have written to the District surveyor to state say that as the room is to be non-habitable you need not, according to Byelaw 12.02, comply with fire regulations relating to the doors on the ground and first floors.)   u/c

run on
The new room will be provided with a half-hour firecheck door.

2. In relation to the cracked plaster in the kitchen, we do not believe the cracks indicate a major problem [as there are not no signs of cracks in the rear wall of the house. [There are two possible explanations for the cracks – they could be due to a general drying out of the plaster after the central heating was installed or they could be associated with war damage when the anti-aircraft batteries were located in your area during the 2nd W. War   NP   [for the house,

put in full

3. All loose or cracked roof tiles will indeed be replaced.

Please let me know if you have any other queries.

Yours sincerely

John Pickering

Assignment 6   (a)   Create a new document and key in the text about checking brakes.

(b)   Save the document.

(c)   Print out one copy,.

CHECKING THE BRAKES   *] embolden heading*

of all

First/ remove one of the wheels and refer to the car handbook for advice on how to slacken the brake shoe adjuster(s). Next, take off the drum by undoing the retaining screws then/ease off by tapping the protruding *[if necessary]* rim, using a hammer and a block of wood. /~~Cean~~ the shiny *[Once freed, clean]* inside surface of the drum with a rag dipped in methylated spirit, and check for scoring. If the face isn't smooth, the drum will have to be replaced.

Next inspect the linings and have them changed if they are loose, oil-fouled, or less than 2 mm thick above the shoe or rivet head.

Slave cylinder   *[no underline — just bold]*

While accessible, examine the slave cylinder and get the rubber dust covers replaced if perished. Also check for hydraulic fluid leaks. If you find any, you will probably need to have the seals inside the cylinder renewed/. If the *[immediately]* car has been standing for a while, another sign of leaking fluid is discolouration at the base of the drum on the outside.

When reassembling, set the brake shoe adjuster(s) to the handbook's recommendation and then repeat the operation on the opposite drum.

Discs and pads

Remove one of the wheels and check the thickness of the pads through the opening in the caliper casing. The recommended minimum will be in the car handbook. If one or both are near the limit, arrange to have the pads changed by an expert.

[run on] Also check both braking surfaces of the disc and if one shows signs of rust, have the brake examined by a garage (a caliper piston may have seized). Ensure too that the disc spins without resistance, and that both faces are smooth. If not, seek garage advice. ~~And examine for oil and hydraulic brake fluid leaks at the base of the assembly.~~

Lastly, replace the wheel and repeat the operation on the other disc brake(s).

Assignment 7

(a)   Recall the text created in the previous assignment.

(b)   There is an additional section called 'The hydraulic system'. Add this to the end of the document.

(c)   To make further editing easier, change the line spacing to double.

(d)   Justify the right margin.

(e)   Number the pages.

(f)   Save this new version (the earlier version is no longer needed).

(g)   Print out one copy.

same as earlier headings

<u>The hydraulic system</u>

regularly

Make a point of inspecting the whole hydraulic system under
the car ~~every/now and then~~. Your life could depend on it.
A typical system starts with the brake pedal, proceeds to
the master cylinder and continues to the roadwheels, for
the most part in small diameter steel tubing. The final   *(see diagram)*
part of the journey to the backplate of each wheel, to
which the slave cylinders are attached, is a flexible hose.

r

The ~~three~~ priorities are to examine for evidence of
hydraulic fluid leaks, corrosion of the steel tubing, and
wear and chafing of the flexible pipes.

Check for leaks: check all joints and T-pieces and ensure
that union nuts are tight. In addition, inspect the
backplates of the roadwheels, including the bleed nipples.

Then examine the steel tubing for signs of serious pitting
and corrosion, paying particular attention to the spots
where the tubing is clipped to the underbody. If securing
clips are made of metal, rapid corrosion can take place in
the area of contact. After this, check the flexible hoses
for fatigue, damage and perishing.

~~Remedial work on any part of the braking system is best
left to a garage.~~

Assignment 8

Three diagrams need to be inserted into the text about checking the brakes (Assignments 6 and 7).

(a)   Based on the information below, insert the necessary vertical space in the text in the appropriate places so that the diagrams can be added at a later stage.

(i)   The first diagram goes in the 'Slave cylinder' section between the two paragraphs. 8 cm will be sufficient.

(ii)   7 cm will be enough for the next diagram which goes in the 'Discs and pads' section at the end—that is, after the last paragraph.

(iii)   The diagram for 'The hydraulic system' needs a space of 10 cm and is to be placed between '...chafing of the flexible pipes.' and the paragraph which begins 'Check for leaks: check...'.

(b) Repaginate, if necessary, and maintain page numbering.

(c) Print out one copy.

Assignment 9

(a) Display the details of the conference programme below as effectively as possible.

(b) Print out two copies.

DESK TOP PUBLISHING
CONFERENCE PROGRAMME } centre +
emboldern

Wednesday, 8 March

16·30	Arrival/Registration	Main Office
18·30	Reception	Bar
19·30	Dinner	Main Hall

Thursday 9 March

08·00	Breakfast	Main Hall
09·00	Welcome address by Chair	Seminar Room 1
09·15	Sandra Woodward "Popular uses of Electronic Publishing"	"
10·05	Coffee	Bar
10·35	Mohammed Sakho "Introducing DTP-management + cost"	Seminar Room 1
11·25	Exhibition Workshop	Seminar Rooms 2 + 3
12·45	Lunch	Main Hall
14·00	Jennifer Barron "The personal computer as a graphic design tool"	Seminar Room 1
14·50	Tea	Bar
15·30	Chair's summary and closing discussion	Seminar Room 1
16·15	Close of conference	

Champion Conference Centre, Champion House, Mary Street,
Stockport, Greater Manchester SK1 3NN
Tel: Greater Manchester (061) 488 3518

Assignment 10

You work for the personnel department at Andrew Crown plc at Marlow House, Church Road, Isleworth, Middlesex.

The people listed below have been shortlisted for the position of Grade II clerical assistant in your organisation.

(a) Compose a letter informing them of the details of their interview, based on the details below.

(i)   The interviews are to be held on the first Thursday of next month.

(ii)   Give each applicant the time of his/her interview. Begin at 2.00 pm and allow twenty minutes for each person. Allow for a break of fifteen minutes at a suitable time so that the interviewing panel can have tea.

(iii)   Candidates should check in at the main reception desk on arrival.

(iv)   The normal procedure is to interview candidates in alphabetical order.

(b)   Save and print out a personalised letter to each applicant.

Applicants for Grade II clerical post

Jan Ellis
48 Nelson Rd
Isleworth
Middlsx

Peter Barclay
201 Lester Road
London SW4

Hugh McQuaid
34 Loughton Road
St. Margarets
Middlsx

Angela Witham
85 Stratford Road
Hounslow
Middlesex

Leroy Brown
23 Grove Square
Walton-on-Thames
Surrey

Claire Edwards
67 The Willows
Willows Lane
Surbiton
Surrey

9   Spreadsheet Assignments

By completing the spreadsheet assignments, students will
demonstrate the ability to:

1   LOAD a spreadsheet program
2   LOAD a spreadsheet model
3   ENTER text
4   ENTER numeric data
5   EDIT entries
6   INSERT columns and rows
7   DELETE columns and rows
8   GENERATE formulae
9   APPLY formulae
10 REPLICATE formulae
11 AMEND formulae
12 CHANGE cell sizes
13 GENERATE 'what...if?' projections
14 SAVE a spreadsheet model
15 PRINT data
16 PRINT model with formulae
17 EXIT from a spreadsheet program

**Objectives covered by
each assignment**

Assignment 1
(1), 3, 4, 8, 9, 13, 14, 15, (17)

Assignment 2
(1), 3, 4, 5, 8, 9, 13, 14, 15, (17)

Assignment 3
(1), 2, 3, 4, 5, 8, 9, 13, 15, 16, (17)

Assignment 4
(1), 3, 4, 8, 9, 10, 12, 13, 14, 15, (17)

Assignment 5
(1), 2, 3, 4, 6, 11, 15, 16, (17)

Assignment 6
(1), 3, 4, 8, 9, 10, 12, 13, 14, 15, (17)

Assignment 7
(1), 2, 3, 4, 7, 8, 9, 15, 16, (17)

Assignment 8
(1), 3, 4, 8, 9, 10, 14, 15, (17)

Assignment 9
(1), 2, 3, 4, 5, 6, 7, 11, 15, (17)

Assignment 10
(1), 3, 4, 8, 9, 13, 15, 16, (17)

Assignment 1

A simple way of estimating the approximate net profit for a sales company for the following year is to subtract the cost of sales from the income generated by projected sales.

(a)   Create a spreadsheet model which will work this out, using a similar layout to the one below.

	amount (pounds)
income	(any figure)
cost	(any figure)
profit	(formula)

(b)   Enter the appropriate formula.
(c)   Assume cost to be 13550.
(d)   Use the model to see what the profit would be if sales generate an income of 25370.
(e)   What would the profit be if the value of sales falls to 14759?
(f)   Save your model and print out a copy.

Assignment 2

(a)   Create a spreadsheet model for a small garage which charges its customers for parts and labour (as shown below). Enter the correct formula for the total cost.

	cost
labour	(any figure)
parts	(any figure)
Total cost	(formula)

(b)   Use your model to work out the following bills:

labour   £25
parts   £62.50

labour   £98
parts   £49.75

(c)   Save the model and print out one of the above examples.

Assignment 3

(a) Recall the garage model you created for the previous assignment. Amend the model so that 15 per cent is added to the total to give a final total which includes VAT.

(b) Use the model to work out the same two bills as above in 2 (b).

(c) Print out one of the examples.

(d) Print out the model showing the *formulae*.

Assignment 4

The formula for converting x degrees fahrenheit into centigrade is $(x - 32)*5/9$.

(a) Create a spreadsheet model which will convert figures from fahrenheit into centigrade.

(b) Check that the formula is correct by entering 50 for the fahrenheit figure. Your model should show that this is equivalent to 10 degrees centigrade.

(c) Create a model, as shown below, which will work out the temperature in degrees centigrade in various locations. You may get more than one figure after the decimal point—there are ways of changing that, but don't worry about it now.

Instead of keying in the formula each time for every location, replicate (that is, copy) the formula for the whole column.

You may need to change the cell size in order to fit in the names of the locations.

	°F	°C
Amsterdam	59	(put in formula)
Athens	71	
Berlin	62	
Brussels	63	
Cardiff	57	
Dublin	59	
Glasgow	58	
London	64	
Madrid	69	
Moscow	57	
New York	69	
Paris	60	
Rome	70	

(d) What is the temperature in degrees centigrade if:

(i) the temperature in Brussels goes up to 66 degrees fahrenheit;

(ii) the temperature in London goes down to 61 degrees fahrenheit.

(e) Leaving in the changes made in (d), add a formula which will work out the average temperature for all the locations in both centigrade and fahrenheit.

(f)   Save and print out the model.

Assignment 5

Recall the weather model created in the previous assignment.

(a)   Insert, in the correct position alphabetically, Istanbul with a temperature of 74 degrees fahrenheit.

(b)   If necessary, amend the formulae to include the new location in the calculation.

(c)   Print out a copy of the model showing the *formulae*.

Assignment 6

(a)   A group of work colleagues have collected £152 to buy a dinner service as a wedding present. The price list for the service is:

item	unit cost (pounds)
large plate	5.95
small plate	4.50
saucer	3.95
teacup	4.35
teapot	8.00
coffee cup	4.45
coffee pot	9.25
sugar bowl	5.50
milk jug	4.10
gravy boat	7.60

(b)   Enter the details on a worksheet. Either change the cell size to accommodate the full description of the items or use suitable abbreviations.

(c)   Add two more columns: one for the number you might buy of each item and one for the cost of that number of items. The last column should therefore contain a formula which multiplies the previous two columns. This formula can be entered for the first item and then replicated for the rest of the column. You will also need a cell for the total cost, that is, the sum of all the entries in the last column.

(d)   What is the total cost if you buy:

6   large plates
6   small plates
6   saucers
6   teacups
1   teapot
1   sugar bowl
1   milk jug

(e)   With the money collected, could you afford the above *plus* 6 coffee cups and a coffee pot?

(f)   Experiment with the figures and see what you can sensibly afford with the money you have collected.

(g)   Save and print out the model which you think is most suitable.

Assignment 7

Recall the dinner service model created in the previous assignment.

(a)   There are no more gravy boats in stock, so delete the appropriate row.

(b)   A discount of 7.5 per cent is now being offered on the dinner service. Enter additional formulae so that the model now displays:

(i)   the total without discount;
(ii)   the total discount;
(iii) the final total.

(c)   Print out a copy of the model which shows the *formulae.*

Assignment 8

Key in the model below which shows the exam results for a group of students.

STUDENT SURNAME	Exam 1	Exam 2	Exam 3	TOTAL	AVERAGE
Armstrong	63	72	59		
Brookman	89	85	79		
Ealing	62	45	58		
Evans	45	54	52		
Grange	59	55	61		
Lambert	89	78	76		
Sampson	32	41	41		
Smart	55	54	51		

TOTAL

AVERAGE

(a)   Fill in the formulae for the totals and averages, using the facility to replicate formulae where appropriate. The last two columns represent the total and average marks for each student and the last two rows represent the total and average marks in the class for each exam.

(b)   Save the model and print out a copy.

Assignment 9

Recall the exam model created in the previous assignment.

(a)   One student—Baker—has been missed out by mistake. Put her in (in the correct position alphabetically). Her results are: 61, 69 and 62.

(b)   The results of another exam—Exam 4—need to be entered they are:

Armstrong	70
Baker	65
Brookman	80
Ealing	60
Evans	59
Grange	58
Lambert	66
Sampson	58
Smart	64

(c) Amend the formulae if necessary to include the new exam.

(d) One student—Sampson—has been transferred to another group. Delete the appropriate row.

(e) Print out a copy of the model.

Assignment 10

You have been offered an interest-free loan of £750 but have to pay an additional charge which varies according to the number of monthly repayments you make (the repayments are of equal amounts).

(a) Create a model which shows the following:

(i)   the amount you wish to borrow;

(ii) the percentage charge made for the loan;

(iii) the number of monthly repayments;

(iv) the value of the charge;

(v)   the total cost of the loan;

(vi) the amount of each monthly repayment.

[The last three should be represented by formulae based on the first three variables.]

The charges for the loan are as follows:

an extra	5%	for	6	equal repayments
	8%		12	
	9%		15	
	15%		24	
	17%		36	

(b) For *each* of the five possible methods of paying for the loan indicated above, how much would you pay **in total** for your loan and how much would you have to pay **each month**?

(c) Save the model and print out a copy of the model showing the formulae.

10   **Database Assignments**

By completing the database assignments, students will demonstrate the ability to:

1 LOAD a database program
2 LOAD an existing database
3 QUERY a database
4 DETERMINE record structure
5 ENTER record structure
6 CREATE database files
   (with alphabetical and numerical fields)
7 ENTER alphabetical and numerical data
8 ADD records
9 DELETE records
10 AMEND records
11 SORT data
    (alphabetically and numerically)
12 SEARCH on up to five criteria to extract data
13 SAVE a database
14 PRINT data
15 PRINT selected fields
16 EXIT from a database program

Objectives covered by each assignment

Assignment 1
(1), 3, 4, 5, 6, 7, 12, 14, (16)

Assignment 2
(1), 3, 4, 5, 6, 7, 11, 12, 14, (16)

Assignment 3
(1), 4, 5, 6, 7, 13, 14, (16)

Assignment 4
(1), 2, 8, 9, 10, 14, 15, (16)

Assignment 5
(1), 4, 5, 6, 7, 11, 12, 13, 15, (16)

Assignment 6
(1), 2, 3, 8, 9, 10, 11, 12, 14, (16)

Assignment 7
(1), 4, 5, 6, 7, 12, 15, (16)

Assignment 8
(1), 3, 4, 5, 6, 7, 9, 12, 13, 14, (16)

Assignment 9
(1), 2, 3, 12, 15, (16)

Assignment 10
(1), 3, 4, 5, 6, 7, 10, 11, 12, 15, (16)

Assignment 1

(a)   Elect one member of your group to write on the board everyone's surname and their zodiac sign.

(b)   Create a database of these details by having two fields in each record:

    NAME
    SIGN

(c)   Search for all those who have the same zodiac sign as you. Make a note of how many there are.

(d)   Print out a hard copy of all the records.

Assignment 2

(a)   Create a database for your record, cassette or book collection, using at least 10 records, each with three fields:

    ARTIST (or AUTHOR)
    TITLE
    YEAR (or production or publication)

(Use the surname for the artist or author.)

(b)   If you do not have any of the above, collect the details of at least 10 records, cassettes or books you would *like* to own.

(c)   Swap with a colleague and look through each other's database on screen. How many of your colleague's records, cassettes or books are older than two years?

(d)   Sort your *own* database so that the artists or authors appear in alphabetical order.

(e)   Print out a copy of all the records.

Assignment 3

The details of a company's car fleet need to be transferred from a card index to a database.

(a)   Look at the cards on pages 57 and 58 and decide on suitable field names for each record. *All* the information needs to be transferred.

(b)   Create the database, enter the data and save it.

(c)   Print out a copy of all the records.

Assignment 4

(a)   Recall the car fleet database created in the previous assignment.

(b)   There have been a number of staff changes. Amend the records accordingly.

Name	Elaine HUNT
Title/Position	MD
Car type	Mercedes
Registration	E 740 TYL

Name	Shelby HARDING
Title/Position	P.A.
Car type	Golf
Registration	D 504 KJN

Name	Alexander HOWARD
Title/Position	Assistant Director
Car type	AUDI QUATRO
Registration	D 966 LFG

Name	John LEIGH
Title/Position	Sales Rep
Car type	Cavalier CD
Registration	E 489 LTJ

Name	Mark CHANG
Title/Position	Sales Rep
Car type	ESCORT
Registration	E 503 BKT

Name	Richard LAWSON
Title/Position	Company Secretary
Car type	Alfa Sud
Registration	D 748 AOC

Name	Kieran Brannigan
Title/Position	Sales Rep
Car type	Escort
Registration	D 532 BLS

Name	Dakshesh KHAN
Title/Position	Sales Rep
Car type	Escort
Registration	C 431 MNN

Name	Lorraine HATCHARD
Title/Position	Executive Director
Car type	Montego
Registration	D 537 STN

Name	Lesley BLETCHWORTH
Title/Position	Sales Rep
Car type	OPEL MANTA
Registration	E 549 CYL

Name	Eleanor HAWKES
Title/Position	Personnel Officer
Car type	Lotus 7
Registration	E214 BJN

Name	Alan BRAIDWOOD
Title/Position	Assistant Director
Car type	Scirocco
Registration	D702 LLK

Name	Kate French
Title/Position	Sales Rep
Car type	Opel Manta
Registration	E960 MMN

Name	Richard BAMBER
Title/Position	Accountant
Car type	Saab
Registration	E400 BCJ

Name	Naomi Sullivan
Title/Position	Assistant Director
Car type	Golf
Registration	E663 FLA

Name	John POLLOCK
Title/Position	Sales Rep
Car type	Cavalier
Registration	E531 FMT

(i)   Alexander Howard has left the company.

(ii)   Lorraine Hatchard has been promoted to Assistant Director and is therefore entitled to a more expensive car. She has been given Mr Howard's car.

(iii)   Two new sales representatives have been recruited: Elaine Gerrard and Michael O'Shea. Ms Gerrard has been given an Opel Manta, registration number E604 CYA and Mr O'Shea a Cavalier CD, registration number E748 BOC.

(iv)   Dak Khan's car—now somewhat old—has been replaced by a Mazda, E805 LYL.

(c)   Print out all the records incorporating the above amendments.

(d)   The Accounts Department needs a list of all the sales representatives who have company cars. Print out the information for them.

Assignment 5   Details of the students listed on page 59, who have just enrolled

in the Business Studies Department at a College of Further
Education, need to be keyed into a new database.

(a)   Create the database with four fields in each record, as
      follows:

         SURNAME
         FORENAME
         COURSE
         MODE

      The abbreviations used are L (Law), A (Accounting), O (Office
      Technology), M (Marketing), F (Full-time), P (Part-time).

      Accounting is offered on a full-time basis only.

      When you have keyed in the data, sort it and make the
      appropriate hard copies so as to provide the following people
      with the information they need.

(b)   Each of the four course tutors needs a list of the details of
      the new students they are to expect on their particular
      course.

(c)   The registrar needs two lists with all the details—one for all
      new full-time students and another for all new part-time
      students.

(d)   The Deputy Head of the Department wants one list of all the
      new students and their details with the surnames in
      alphabetical order.

(e)   Save the database.

Alan Rider   O/F
Sophie Denison O/F
Lester John *   P/M
Browjing Margaret L/F
Gina Torselli L/P
Helen DEARDS   A
Graham Harding M/P
Bernard Harris   A
Adie Patel   L/F
(Ayshe) Grant M/P
Linda Evans M/F

Graham OWEN   O/P
Taylor Lisa   O/P
Tracey Khan   M/P

* John is
  surname

AYSHE

Assignment 6   Recall the student database created in the previous assignment and update accordingly.

(a)   Four new students have enrolled:

Maggie Walker and Peter Lachowicz for Accounting
Simon Dorrell for Marketing, full-time
Mike Kelley for Law, full-time.

(b)   Ayshe Grant has changed her mind and wants to do Office Technology instead of Marketing. She still prefers to attend part-time.

(c)   Sophie Denis has decided to go to another college.

(d)   Print out one updated copy of all the new students (in alphabetical order) for the Deputy Head.

(e)   Enrolments for the full-time marketing course are low so far this year. How many of the new students have chosen this option?

Assignment 7   (a)   Transfer the employment details from the cards shown below, opposite and on page 62 to a database using suitable field names.

(b)   You have requests from five different companies who want staff from your agency. Prepare a print-out of possible employees for each of them.

(i)   A public relations company wants someone with fast keyboarding skills—other details immaterial.

(ii)   A firm of solicitors wants someone with keyboarding skills who has a reasonable knowledge of computers.

(iii)   An insurance company wants someone who has had office experience and can type. Information Technology skills would be an advantage.

(iv)   A French speaker with Information Technology skills is needed by an export company. Must be over 25 years old.

Name	Rebecca Marsh
Address	14 Ravenscourt Road
	Leigh-on-Sea, Essex
Phone	(0702) 48310 Age 22
IT lit	yes/no Keybding 40 wpm
Office exp	yes/no Sh/h yes/no
Languages	/

Name	Elaine Thompson
Address	19 Claythorpe Drive
	London EC4
Phone	620 8443 Age 19
IT lit	yes/no Keybding 60 wpm
Office exp	yes/no Sh/h yes/no
Languages	/

Name	Adrienne Dodd
Address	58 Thorpe Park Drive
	Westcliff, Essex
Phone	(0702) 92497 Age 29
IT lit	yes/no Keybding 55 wpm
Office exp	yes/no Sh/h yes/no
Languages	—

Name	Michael LEWIS
Address	58 Burroughs Road
	London SW4
Phone	673 9954 Age 20
IT lit	yes/no Keybding 40 wpm
Office exp	yes/no Sh/h yes/no
Languages	—

Name	Olwen Davies
Address	22 Eastleigh House
	Faversham Road, Basildon, Essex
Phone	(0268) 33352 Age 30
IT lit	yes/no Keybding 55 wpm
Office exp	yes/no Sh/h yes/no
Languages	FRENCH

Name	Doran Gray
Address	18 Marsh Way
	Bishop's Stortford
Phone	(0279) 31002 Age 17
IT lit	yes/no Keybding 30 wpm
Office exp	yes/no Sh/h yes/no
Languages	—

Name	Helen Lambert
Address	14 Blewbury Street
	London EC2
Phone	443 8157 Age 40
IT lit	yes/no Keybding 50 wpm
Office exp	yes/no Sh/h yes/no
Languages	FRENCH, GERMAN

Name	Odile Gray
Address	15 Parkway
	Harlow, Essex
Phone	(0279) 02451 Age 33
IT lit	yes/no Keybding 55 wpm
Office exp	yes/no Sh/h yes/no
Languages	FRENCH

Name	Frank Johnson
Address	58 Aberfeldy House
	Tilbury
Phone	(03752) 21994 Age 40
IT lit	yes/no Keybding 60 wpm
Office exp	yes/no Sh/h yes/no
Languages	—

Name	Sheila Patel
Address	55 Healey Estate
	Southend, Essex
Phone	(0702) 21134 Age 17
IT lit	yes/no Keybding 30 wpm
Office exp	yes/no Sh/h yes/no
Languages	—

Name	Helen Tsiakolis
Address	24 Clarence Way
	Chelmsford, Essex
Phone (0245) 93112	Age 42
IT lit yes/no	Keybding 45 wpm
Office exp yes/no	Sh/h yes/no
Languages	

Name	Lesley Brown
Address	Meredith House, Long Walk,
	Rainham, Essex
Phone (04027) 33651	Age 29
IT lit yes/no	Keybding 65 wpm
Office exp yes/no	Sh/h yes/no
Languages	GERMAN, SPANISH

Name	Oliver Smith
Address	48 Nordelph Road
	Colchester, Essex
Phone (0206) 42215	Age 25
IT lit yes/no	Keybding 35 wpm
Office exp yes/no	Sh/h yes/no
Languages	

Name	Lilly Tse
Address	15 Bolton Close
	Leigh-on-Sea, Essex
Phone (0702) 91675	Age 34
IT lit yes/no	Keybding 50 wpm
Office exp yes/no	Sh/h yes/no
Languages	FRENCH, ITALIAN

Name	Frances Silverman
Address	22 Baron's Court, Baron
	Road, Braintree, Essex
Phone (0376) 45219	Age 21
IT lit yes/no	Keybding 35 wpm
Office exp yes/no	Sh/h yes/no
Languages	FRENCH

(v) A 'mature' person is required by a local firm. Must have IT skills, office experience and good typing. Shorthand would be useful but is not essential.

Assignment 8

(a) As an employee of an estate agents in a fashionable part of London, you have been asked to transfer the details of properties for sale (as shown on pages 64, 65 and 66) to a database using the fields listed below:

                    REF NO
                    AREA
                    PRICE
                    HS/FLAT
                    BEDS
                    RECEPS
                    GARDEN

[Ignore any other information given about the properties.]

(b)   A colleague from another branch in your area has had a lot
      of requests for flats and asks for the following information:

      (i)   How many flats do you have for sale?
      (ii)   Are there any for less than £75,000? If so, how many?
      (iii) Are there any for less than £75,00 with two or more
             bedrooms? If so, how many?
      (iv)   Are there any for less than £75,000 with two or more
             bedrooms *and* a garden?

(c)   As well as providing the above information for your
      colleague, prepare a print-out of all the flats you have for sale
      (with all their details).
(d)   Property ref. no. 005 has been sold. Take it off the records.
(e)   Save the database.

Assignment 9

Using the estate agent database created in the previous assignment,
deal with the following enquiries by printing out details of any
suitable properties for each customer:

(a)   Mr Parkinson wants a property in SW19 with five or more
      bedrooms.
(b)   Ms Kelly is looking for a one bedroom flat in SW20.
(c)   Ms Evans wants a three bedroom house with a garden for
      under £95,000.
(d)   Mr and Mrs Cooper want a four bedroom house with two
      receptions and a garden in SW19 or SW20.

Assignment 10

Amin's Newsagents is situated at the corner of St Mathew's Road
and High Street. They deliver newspapers in the area shown in the
map on page 67. Mr Amin has decided to transfer the details of
deliveries to a database on his microcomputer to make ordering
and delivering easier.

(a)   Transfer the details on page 67 to a database, using suitable
      field names.
(b)   Amend the database to take account of the fact that the

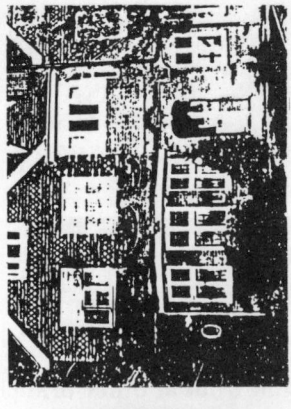

4 SW19 £555,000
Large character house—fantastic views over common, 7 bedrooms, 3 bathrooms, 3 large reception rooms, breakfast room, kitchen, utility room, cellar, garden

8 SW19 £299,000
Double fronted detached house between park and common. 5 beds, 2 bathrooms, oak panelled hall, 2 receptions, kitchen/breakfast room, utility room, playroom, gas CH, beautiful garden

3 SW20 £127,000
Four bedrooms, bathroom, sep WC, two receps, fitted kitchen, 110 ft garden

7 SW19 £190,000
Four bedrooms, bathroom, sep WC, 2 large receps, 21 ft kitchen, 85 ft garden

2 SW19 £75,950
Flat, two large bedrooms, lounge, kitchen, garden

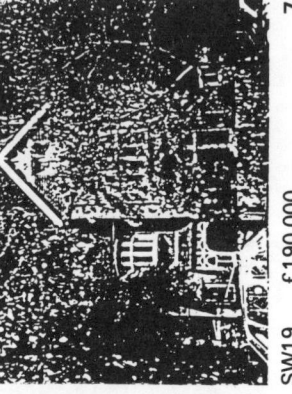

6 SW20 £52,000
First floor flat. One bedroom, kitchen, lounge. Parking space

1 SW19 £89,000
House, three good bedrooms, bathroom, sep WC, 2 receps, kitchen, garden, new roof, gas CH

5 SW4 £159,000
House, four beds, bathroom, sep WC, living room, dining room, kitchen/breakfast room, 60 ft garden

16 £165,00

SW19 House within easy reach of town centre and station. 4 beds, 2 receps, conservatory, kitchen, bathroom, sep WC, garden (*courtesy of Bazin Estate Agents*)

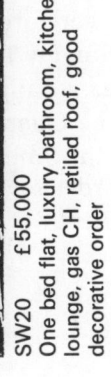

12 £95,000

SW19 Garden level flat near to park. 2 beds, 1 recep, kitchen and bathroom, gas CH and garden

15 £195,000

SW20 Large 1930s-built house, 3 beds, bath, 2 receps, cloakroom, gas CH, garage, 180 ft south-facing garden

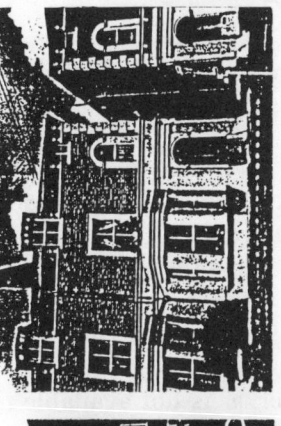

11 £450,500

SW20 Immaculate house, spectacular views, 4 bedrooms, 2 bathrooms, 3 reception rooms, kitchen, garage, garden, beautiful terrace

14 £124,000

SW20 Four bed house, luxury bathroom, shower room, 2 receps, fitted kitchen, double glazing, garden, garage

10 £157,000

SW19 Four beds, bathroom, sep WC, living room, dining room, kitchen, gas CH, double glazing, garden

13 £85,000

SW12 Spacious 2 bed flat in excellent decorative order. Bathroom, WC, lounge, gas CH, original fireplaces, stripped doors, private rear garden

9 £55,000

SW20 One bed flat, luxury bathroom, kitchen, lounge, gas CH, retiled roof, good decorative order

65

SW12   £61,000   **17**
2 bed flat, bathroom, lounge, kitchen,
fitted carpets

SW12   £131,000   **18**
Cottage-style terraced house,
3 bedrooms, luxury bathroom, lounge,
kitchen with oven and hob, fully carpeted

SW20   £65,000   **19**
Ground floor flat in good decorative
order close to station. 2 beds, lounge,
kitchen, bathroom, **own** garden

SW20   £102,000   **20**
Flat in pleasant block. 2 beds, large
L-shaped reception room, bathroom,
kitchen, gas CH, garage space

family at 98 Honeybrook Road have changed from the *Times* to the *Guardian*.

(c)   The two students who deliver the papers each morning take one side of High Street each. Print out two lists—one for each of them with the details of which papers they have to deliver to which house.

(d)   The *Observer* is not available next week and there is not enough time to ask which papers people want instead. Therefore, Mr Amin has decided to deliver the *Sunday Telegraph* to those who take the *Telegraph* or *Times* as a daily and the *Sunday Times* to those who take the *Guardian* or the *Independent*. How many more of each (the *Sunday Telegraph* and the *Sunday Times*) will he have to order for next week?

(e)   Print out all the records.

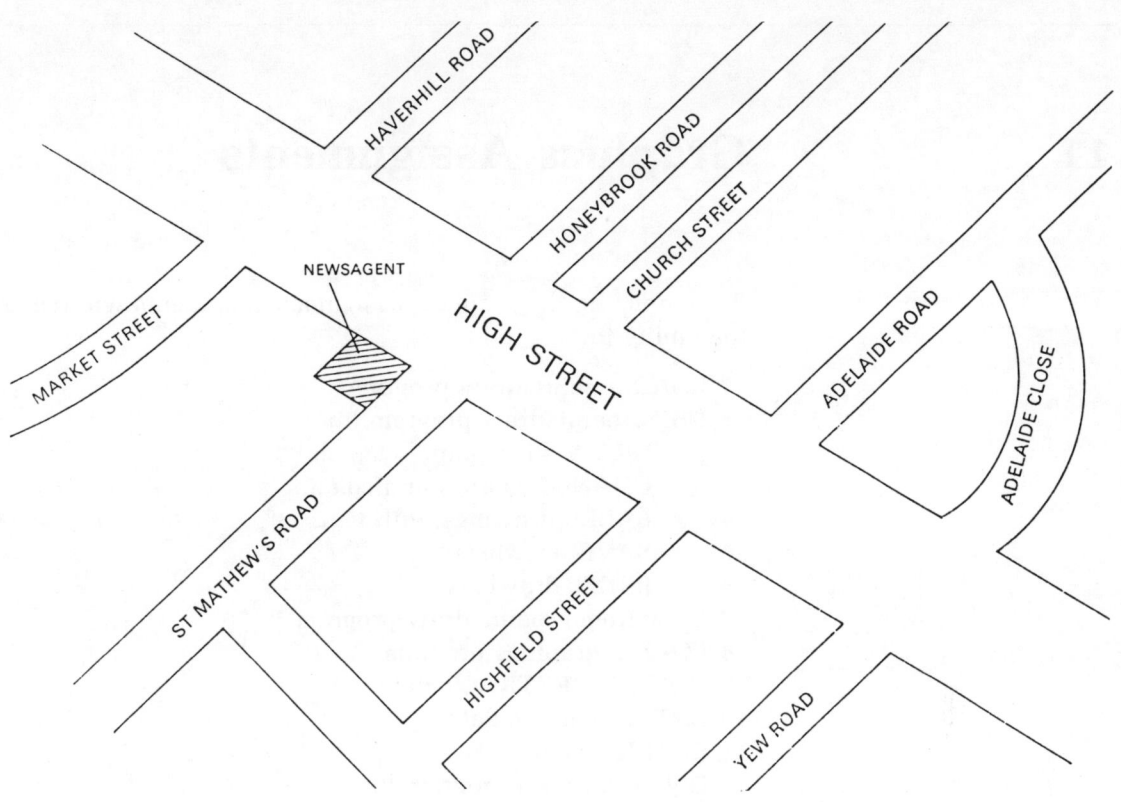

NAME	ADDRESS	DAILY	SUNDAY
HOLLAND	48 Honeybrook	Guardian	Observer
ESPOSITO	9 Highfield	Sun	News of the World
CLARENCE	28 Church St.	Times	Sunday Times
CLARK	105 Market Street	Sun	N of the W
WICKHAM	15 Highfield	Mirror	News on Sunday
PATEL	9 St. Mathews	Independent	Observer
CULE	35 St. Mathews	Independent	News on Sunday
ROSENBERG	15 Yew Rd	Guardian	Observer
LAWRENCE	65 Highfield	Times	S. Times
FAHED	15 Church Street	Telegraph	S. Telegraph
PRITCHARD	61 Haverhill	Sun	S. Mirror
THORBES	10 Adelaide Road	Sun	News of the World
PAGE	21 Market Street	Independent	Observer
MUDGE	1 Adelaide Close	Mirror	News on Sunday
TORTELLI	18 Market	Times	Observer
HILL	98 Honeybrook	Times	S. Times
TOWERS	6 Yew Rd	Sun	Sunday People
FURNIVAL	8 Highfield	Independent	Observer

11 Graphics Assignments

By completing the graphics assignments, students will demonstrate the ability to:

1 LOAD a paint/draw program
   USE a paint/draw program to:
2   DRAW shapes and symbols
3   CHANGE shapes and colours
4   LABEL drawings with text
5   SAVE drawings
6   PRINT drawings
7 EXIT from a paint/draw program
8 LOAD a graphics program
9 COLLECT/EXTRACT data
10 ENTER numeric data
11 ENTER labels
   USE a graphics program to:
12   PRODUCE pie charts from given data
13   PRODUCE bar charts/histograms from given data
14   PRODUCE line graphs from given data
15   LABEL graphs/charts
16   PRODUCE graphs/charts from formulae
17   SAVE graphs/charts
18   PRINT graphs/charts
19 EXIT from a graphics program

Objectives covered by each assignment

Assignment 1
(1), 2, 3, 4, 5, 6, (7)

Assignment 2
(8), 9, 10, 11, 12, 15, 17, 18, (19)

Assignment 3
(8), 10, 11, 13, 15, 17, 18, (19)

Assignment 4
(8), 10, 11, 14, 15, 17, 18, (19)

Assignment 5
(8), 10, 11, 15, 16, 18, (19)

Assignment 1   (a)   Using a paint/draw package, design a new logo for your workplace, college or school.

(b)   Experiment with shapes and colours until you produce a version you are satisfied with.

(c)   Use text to label your design with your name at the top or bottom of the page.

(d)   Save the design.

(e)   Print out one copy.

Assignment 2   (a)   Find out which type of transport people in your group use to travel to and from work, college or school. Elect one member to write the information on the board using headings such as:

   foot
   bus
   train
   bicycle
   car

(b)   Use the data to produce a pie chart to show how many people use each type of transport.

(c)   Label the pie chart appropriately.

(d)   Save the chart.

(e)   Print out one copy.

Assignment 3   The data below relates to populations in ten of the West African Republics.

(a)   Use the data to produce a histogram, with the title 'West African Republics'.

(b)   Put the republics in alphabetical order.

(c)   On the population axis use a scale of 1:10 million, and label it appropriately. On the other axis, some of the names may need to be abbreviated.

(d)   Save the histogram and print out one copy.

Mauritania	1,290,000
Mali	5,561,000
Senegal	4,315,000
Guinea	4,312,000
Sierra Leone	2,861,000
Liberia	1,669,000
Upper Volta	5,737,000
Ivory Coast	5,897,000
Ghana	9,607,000
Togo	2,117,000

Note: not all the states are included and the figures are approximate.

Assignment 4

In terms of height, female and male babies grow at different rates, and from different starting points, according to the figures below which show national averages in the UK.

(a)   Use the data to produce either:

(i)   one graph showing two lines—one for girls and the other for boys, or

(ii)   two separate line graphs—one for girls and one for boys.

(b)   Label the line graph(s) with 'Age (in months)' on one axis and 'Height (in cm)' on the other.

(c)   Save and print out one copy (or one copy of each graph).

Age in months	Girls' height (cm)	Boys' height (cm)
0 (birth)	52	54
3	58	60
6	64	66
9	69	71
12	73	75
18	80	81.5
24	85	86.5

Assignment 5

The formula for converting x degrees fahrenheit into centigrade is $(x - 32) * 5/9$.

(a)   Use this formula to produce a line graph with degrees centigrade on one axis and degrees fahrenheit on the other.

Use a range of 0–50 for the centigrade axis and 40–120 for the fahrenheit axis.

(b)   Print out the graph.

12   Videotex Assignments

By completing the videotex assignments, students will demonstrate the ability to:

1 LOG ON to a viewdata/teletext system
2 TRACE pages on a specific topic
  USE a local viewdata system to:
3   ENTER pages
4   EDIT pages
5   ROUTE pages
6   CHANGE the routeing of pages
7   COMPOSE new pages
8   COMPOSE new pages, using techniques such as:

- graphics
- coloured text
- background filling
- flashing characters
- double-height characters

9   SAVE pages
10   PRINT pages
11   PRINT routeing information
12 LOG OFF from a viewdata/teletext system

Objectives covered by each assignment

Assignment 1
(1), 2, (10), (12)

Assignment 2
(1), 3, 5, 7, 8, 10, (12)

Assignment 3
(1), 3, 5, 7, 8, 9, 10, 11, (12)

Assignment 4
(1), 2, 3, 4, 5, 6, 7, 8, 9, 10, 11, (12)

Assignment 5
(1), 2, 3, 4, 5, 7, 8, 9, 10, 11, (12)

Assignment 1

You plan to travel from your home to Paris on the first Monday of next month for a meeting at lunch time. You intend to stay for two nights.

(a)   Use a viewdata/teletext system to help you plan your trip.

Use any relevant information which is available on your system for example:

flight timetables
rates of exchange
train times to and from airport
weather forecasts
accommodation

(There may well be other useful topics.)

(b)   Print out, or make a note of, as much relevant information as possible.

Assignment 2

(a)   Look up, using a teletext system, newspapers or magazines, what is on TV next Friday evening. Choose what you think will be the best programme on each channel and create your own 'Preview Special' on a local viewdata system. Route your information as indicated below:

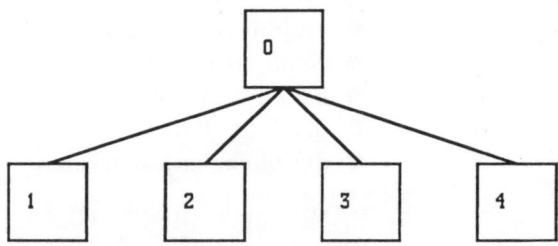

Key in the details for page 0:

PREVIEW SPECIAL

Friday (date)
1 BBC1
2 BBC2
3 ITV
4 Channel 4

Press a Number

(b)   In pages 1, 2, 3 and 4 put in the programme of your choice. Keep the details brief so that everything fits on to one screen 'page'. Put 'Press 0 for main menu' at the bottom of each page.

(c)   Make your presentation as effective as possible using whatever techniques are available (for example, graphics, different colours, flashing or double-height characters).

(d)   Print out the pages.

(e)   Swap over with colleagues and look at their 'Preview Specials'. Do you agree with their choice?

Assignment 3

Employees at Meredith's Advertising Agency read the company's monthly newsletter on their local viewdata system.

The tree diagram below shows how the pages of next month's newsletter is to be routed.

(a) Enter the details (given below and on pages 74 and 75) accordingly.

Make the colour and background filling of page 0 different from those of the other pages.

(b) Save the pages.

(c) Print out the pages, including the routeing information.

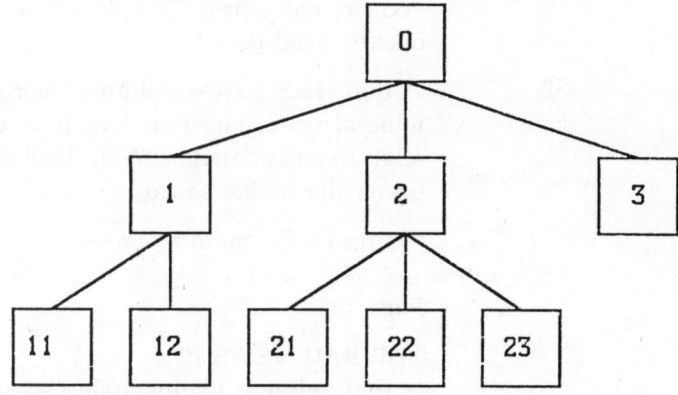

Page 0

This month's in-house News
1 Company performance
2 Staffing
3 Social events

Press a number

Page 1

COMPANY PERFORMANCE
11 Good News
12 Bad News

Press 0 for main menu

Page 2

STAFFING
21 Staff leaving
22 Staff arriving
23 Other staff news

Press 0 for main menu

Page 3

SOCIAL EVENTS
Only one event to note. There will be a presentation on the
25th to Eileen Robey (see page 21). Everyone is welcome.
Come along to her office after work, where drinks and snacks
will be available.

Press 0 for main menu

Page 11

THE GOOD NEWS IS...
...that since the last newsletter we've taken on another
sixteen major projects with seven of them coming from new
clients. Well done!

...that B&B have attributed their 35% increase in sales of
mineral water last year largely to our successful TV
advertising campaign. Well done again! A letter from B&B is
up on the notice board

Press 0 for main menu

Page 12

THE BAD NEWS IS...
...that, while it is obviously necessary to take clients out to
lunch, some people seem to see it as an excuse to imbibe
excessive quantities of alcohol. Please note that in future the
matter will *not* be treated lightly.

Press 0 for main menu

Page 21

STAFF LEAVING
Eileen Robey, from accounts, is leaving us at the end of this
month after three years at Merediths. Many thanks Eileen for
all your hard work and enthusiasm. We shall all miss you.
Good luck in the new job.

See page 3 for details of her farewell gathering.

Press 0 for main menu

Page 22

STAFF ARRIVING
Welcome to Jan Page who will be joining us at the beginning
of next month as an Administrative Assistant in Marketing.
Jan brings to Merediths a wealth of experience and expertise,
especially with computers. She'll be responsible for expanding

and maintaining the database of clients and projects as well as performing a range of administrative tasks.

Press 0 for main menu

Page 23

OTHER STAFF NEWS
As most of you know, congratulations are in order for William Branson on becoming a father. Baby daughter Emma was born on the 3rd and weighed in at 8lb 3oz. Congratulations too, William, on being the first male at Merediths to take advantage of our new arrangements for paternity leave!

We wish William and his wife much happiness (and sleep!)

Press 0 for main menu

Assignment 4   Make the following amendments to the Meredith's newsletter:

(a)   The date of Eileen's farewell has been changed to the 27th. Amend the appropriate page.

(b)   Using the graphics facility, design a tick on the 'Good News' page and a cross on the 'Bad News' page.

(c)   Swap pages 21 and 22 so that 'Staff arriving' comes before 'Staff leaving'. Two other pages will need editing as a result of this change.

(d)   Create a new page—page 4—and call it TALKS. Compose the page, using the same layout as for the other pages. Remind everyone that on the 23rd at 5.30 pm Dr Leaming will be giving a talk on 'The Ethics of Advertising'. Urge everyone to attend (arriving on time) and to participate in the discussion which will follow the talk. The talk will last for about 40 minutes.

Remember to amend page 0.

(e)   Save the pages.

(f)   Print out the pages, including routeing information.

Assignment 5   (a)   In groups of two, or more, create and compose a newsletter for your department, workplace, college, school or society, using real news and events. As well as gathering material yourself, ask others to contribute information or even advertisements.

(b)   Swap with other groups and read their newsletters.

(c)   Save the pages.

(d)   Print out the pages, including the routeing information.

13   Business Accounting Assignments

By completing the business accounting assignments, students will demonstrate the ability to:

1 LOAD an appropriate program
2 LOAD an existing file
3 CREATE a file
4 ENTER records
5 ADD records
6 DELETE records
7 AMEND records
8 SAVE a file
9 PRINT data
10 PRINT selected data
11 PRODUCE a report on specified information
12 BACK-UP files
13 EXIT from the program

Objectives covered by each assignment

Assignment 1
(1), 3, 4, 8, 9, 10, 11, (13)

Assignment 2
(1), 2, 7, 8, 9, 11, 12, (13)

Assignment 3
(1), 2, 5, 7, 8, 9, 11, (13)

Assignment 4
(1), 3, 4, 8, 9, 11, (13)

Assignment 5
(1), 2, 5, 6, 7, 9, 10, 11, (13)

Assignment 1

File-It-Away is a mail order company which provides files for businesses. All customers have accounts and orders have to be in multiples of ten.

Four types of files are sold and each type is available in four colours—black, blue, red and green:

1 Box files in A4 size
2 Box files in foolscap size
3 Lever arch files in A4 size
4 Lever arch files in foolscap size

The stock situation as of yesterday is:

Product code	Cost (£)	Selling price* (£)	No. in stock	Re-order level	Product description
BA1	5.00	5.75	250	400	Box A4 black
BA2	5.00	5.75	290	400	Box A4 blue
BA3	5.00	5.75	730	300	Box A4 red
BA4	5.00	5.75	620	300	Box A4 green
BF1	6.50	7.99	580	300	Box foolscap black
BF2	6.50	7.99	440	300	Box foolscap blue
BF3	6.50	7.99	470	250	Box foolscap red
BF4	6.50	7.99	610	250	Box foolscap green
LA1	5.00	6.50	970	500	Lever A4 black
LA2	5.00	6.50	740	500	Lever A4 blue
LA3	5.00	6.50	320	400	Lever A4 red
LA4	5.00	6.50	630	400	Lever A4 green
LF1	6.00	7.20	390	500	Lever foolscap black
LF2	6.00	7.20	840	500	Lever foolscap blue
LF3	6.00	7.20	1010	400	Lever foolscap red
LF4	6.00	7.20	960	400	Lever foolscap green

*Excluding VAT.

(a)   Create a file in a stock control program and enter the details above, using a layout appropriate for the package.

(b)   Save the file.

(c)   Produce and print out a report listing all stock details as of today.

(d)   Produce and print out a report for any products where the number in stock is below the re-order level for that product.

Assignment 2

(a)   Recall the stock control file created in the previous assignment.

To order files, customers fill in order forms and post them, or they can telephone their order direct in which case a File-It-Away employee fills in the same form.

(b)   Amend the entries according to today's transactions (see completed order forms on pages 78, 79 and 80).

(c)   Produce and print out a report listing all stock details as of today.

(d)   Save the amended file.

(e)   Make a back-up copy of the updated file.

Assignment 3

File-It-Away intend to introduce a new lever arch file on a trial basis to see how it sells. The file comes in both sizes (A4 and foolscap) and is patterned in colour rather than plain (500 of each size have been purchased).

FILE-IT-AWAY
Harrigan House
Harrigan Square
Sheffield
Yorkshire
Tel 0742 887517

ORDER FORM   DATE ....

code	description	quantity	unit cost	price (£)
BA2	Blue A4 Box	30	5.75	172.50
BA3	Red A4 Box	70	5.75	402.50
TOTAL				575.00
VAT at 15%				86.25
TOTAL INC VAT				661.25

Customer name ...... Viney. Watson + Drew ....

Customer account code ...... VWD ....

FILE-IT-AWAY
Harrigan House
Harrigan Square
Sheffield
Yorkshire
Tel 0742 887517

ORDER FORM   DATE ....

code	description	quantity	unit cost	price (£)
BA3	Box files - red	100	5.75	575
BA4	Box files - green	100	5.75	575
TOTAL				1150
VAT at 15%				172.50
TOTAL INC VAT				1322.50

Customer name ...... Harlands International Group ....

Customer account code ...... H.I.G ....

FILE-IT-AWAY
Harrigan House
Harrigan Square
Sheffield
Yorkshire
Tel 0742 887517

ORDER FORM   DATE ....

code	description	quantity	unit cost	price (£)
LF4	LEVER ARCH GREEN FOOLSCAP	50	7.20	360
TOTAL				360
VAT at 15%				54
TOTAL INC VAT				414

Customer name   Mc Farlanes ....

Customer account code ...... MCF ....

FILE-IT-AWAY
Harrigan House
Harrigan Square
Sheffield
Yorkshire
Tel 0742 887517

ORDER FORM   DATE ....

code	description	quantity	unit cost	price (£)
LA 1	BLACK LEVER ARCH FILES	20	£6.50	£130
LA 3	RED LEVER ARCH FILES	20	£6.50	£130
TOTAL				£260
VAT at 15%				39
TOTAL INC VAT				£299

Customer name NOTS TRAINING CONSORTIUM ....

Customer account code ...... NOTS ....

FILE-IT-AWAY
Harrigan House
Harrigan Square
Sheffield
Yorkshire
Tel 0742 887517

ORDER FORM   DATE ....

code	description	quantity	unit cost	price (£)
LF2	BLUE F/S	150	7.20	1080
	LEVER ARCH			
	FILES			
TOTAL				1080
VAT at 15%				162
TOTAL INC VAT				1242

Customer name *BROADS FREEZER SUPPLIES*

Customer account code *BFS*

FILE-IT-AWAY
Harrigan House
Harrigan Square
Sheffield
Yorkshire
Tel 0742 887517

ORDER FORM   DATE ....

code	description	quantity	unit cost	price (£)
BA1	BLACK A4 BOX	50	5.75	287.50
BF1	BLACK F/S BOX	50	7.99	399.50
LA1	BLACK A4 L/A	50	6.50	325
LF1	BLACK F/S L/A	50	7.20	360
TOTAL				1372.00
VAT at 15%				205.80
TOTAL INC VAT				1577.80

Customer name .... *MAJOR FOOD GROUP* ....

Customer account code ...... *MFG* ....

(a)   Recall the database file used in the previous assignment and enter the details of the new products, using suitable codes and product descriptions. The cost and retail price are the same as the other lever arch files. The re-order level for each should be 200.

(b)   Change the re-order level of BF3 and BF4 to 300.

(c)   The retail prices for BF1/2/3/4 need to be increased to £8.20 as the cost of these products has gone up to £6.75. Amend the details accordingly.

(d)   Save the updated file.

(e)   Print out a report of all stock details.

Assignment 4

(a)   Using a sales ledger program, create accounts for six File-It-Away customers (see list below). Give each customer a credit limit of £1000—if the program has this facility—and assume that there is no amount outstanding for any of these customers.

(b)   From the completed order forms used in the previous assignment, post details of those transactions to a sales ledger file.

(c)   Prepare and print out a report of the account balances for each customer.

(d)   Save the file.

File-It-Away customers

account code	company name and address
NOT	NOTS Training Consortium, Sandwell House, Mark Road, Surbiton, Surrey. Tel. 01–546 72231
HIG	Harlands International Group, Leverman Buildings, Meredith Road, Birmingham. Tel. 021–445 19542
MFG	Major Ford Group PLC, 141–149 Highcross Road, Edinburgh. Tel. 031–589 64444
BFS	Broads Freezer Supplies, Maplin Road, Belfast. Tel. 0232 85541
MCF	McFarlanes, Cranbury Estate, Hyde Road, Sheffield. Tel. 0742 299812
VWD	Viney, Watson and Drew, Brooklands Group, Ramsay Road, St Pauls, Bristol. Tel. 0272 311591

Assignment 5

(a)   Recall the file created in the previous assignment.

(b)   McFarlanes have ordered another 50 foolscap green lever arch files. Post details of this sale to the sales ledger file.

(c)   Two new customers have opened accounts with File-It-Away. They are:

Cross & Barrows Solicitors   LMN Products PLC
Lambeth Road   Everton House
Hillhead   Gosforth
Glasgow   Newcastle

Tel. 041–248 6689   Tel. 0290 0661943

Create accounts for them allowing each a credit limit of £500. Use suitable customer account codes.

(d)   Harlands International Group have gone bankrupt. Delete their account.

(e)   MFG have requested an increase in its credit limit to 1750, which File-It-Away have agreed to. Make the necessary amendment.

(f)   Prepare and print out an updated report of the account balances for each customer.

(g)   Prepare and print out a report of McFarlanes' account history.

(h)   Prepare and print out a report of any customers who have exceeded their credit limit.

PART III

INTEGRATED ASSIGNMENTS

Film Club Network (FCN)
New Office Technology Exhibition (NOTE)
Technical and Scientific Translation (TEST)

By completing the above three integrated assignments, students will demonstrate the ability to:

(a) Prepare and produce word-processed text.
(b) Structure a database and use its facilities to extract and present data.
(c) Create a spreadsheet model, enter data and formulae, and use a model to produce information which assists problem-solving.
(d) Create, route and enter viewdata pages.
(e) Prepare and produce a graphical representation of information from numerical source data.
(f) Incorporate graphical representations into word-processed text (either electronically, if possible, or manually if not).
(g) Follow instructions for the collation and presentation of material which has been prepared using a variety of information technology facilities.

14   Film Club Network

Database

Below is a list of members who have joined FCN (Film Club Network) this month.

Mrs Glenda Brookman, 21 Dowry Rd, New Malden (senior citizen)
Jeremy Lock, 18 Vernon Mansions, Bark Lane, Guildford (student)
Gill Webb, 45 Great Lancing Street, Guildford (student)
Alison Orton, 25 Edmund Road, Mitcham (ordinary)
Andrew McBeth, 88 Keele Road, Morden (unwaged)
Miss Elaine Smith, 12 Hitchin Lane, Kingston (ordinary)
Mr Bracknell, 98 Elgin House, Elgin Road, New Malden (senior citizen)
Ms Anderson, 21 Royal Rise, Kingston (student)
Graham Wallis, 108 Market Place, Hampton (unwaged)
Paul Thomas, 6a Lark Way, New Malden (student)
Ms B Hawkes, 12 Common Rise, Tooting (ordinary)
G Hunt, Pembury House, Jutland Rd, Mitcham (senior citizen)
Laurence Crow, 45 Park View, Richmond (ordinary)
Ms Price, 19 Queens Road, Twickenham (student)
Chris Walker, 102 Sentry Square, St Magarets (unwaged)

(a) Transfer their details on to a database file using the following fields:

> NAME
> ADDRESS
> CATEGORY

CATEGORY refers to whether or not they are:

(1) ordinary members
(2) students
(3) senior citizens
(4) unwaged.

(b) Print out a list of new members in alphabetical order of surnames.

(c) Print out four separate lists—one for each category of new member.

Graphics

Use an appropriate program to produce

(a) A graphical representation of the different categories of FCN members who joined this month.

85

(b) A graphical representation of the different categories of the total FCN membership. Current membership, including this month's new members, is as follows:

Ordinary member	325
Student	272
Senior Citizen	96
Unwaged	103

(c) Print out one copy of each.

Spreadsheet

Membership fees for FCN are as follows:

Ordinary member	£59 per annum
Student	£35 per annum
Senior citizen or unwaged	£5 per annum

(a) Create a spreadsheet model which can be used to calculate (b) below.

(b) Print out clearly labelled models showing:

   (i) what the total income this year will be, given the current membership figures (see graphics for numbers);

   (ii) what the total income will be next year if the current total membership increases by 10 per cent;

   (iii) what the total income will be next year if the current total membership increases by 12 per cent.

(c) Print out the model showing the formulae.

Videotex

Transfer details of this week's films (see pages 87 and 88) on to a local viewdata system and route the pages as indicated below. Display and present the information as effectively as possible.

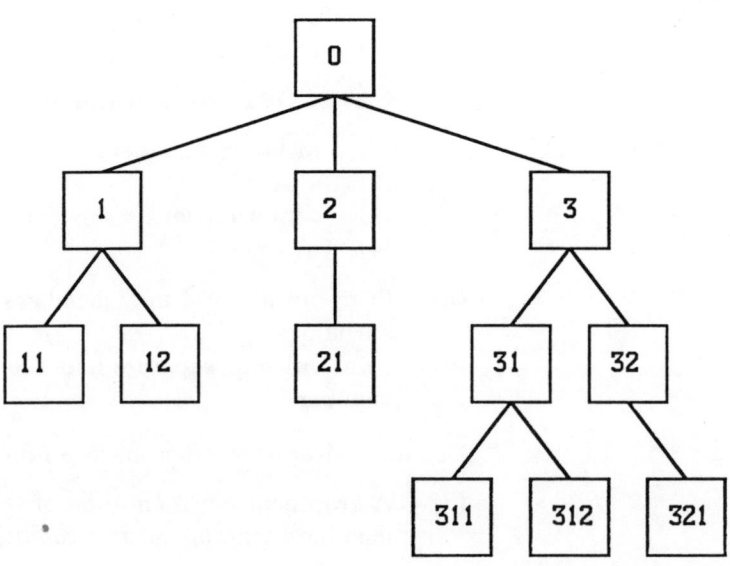

FCN—THIS WEEK'S FILMS

Serious films

STATION SIX—SAHARA   On an isolated oil pipeline station, five men bicker and squabble in the heat and isolation. Then blonde siren Carroll Baker crashes into their lives.
UK 1963   Dir. Seth Holt   Monday 7 pm

NIGHT AND CITY   A lurid, violent saga of gangland power struggles over all-in wrestling. Richard Widmark as a Soho wide boy and Gene Tierney as his Cockney singer girlfriend.
UK 1950   Dir. Jules Dassin   Saturday 7 pm

Light films

HANNAH AND HER SISTERS   Woody Allen's comedy of Manhattan manners turning on three sisters and their men, with Allen playing the hypochondriac and Mia Farrow and Michael Caine giving fine performances.
USA 1986   Dir. Woody Allen   Friday 7.30 pm

Foreign films

French

SHOOT THE PIANIST (Tirez sur le pianiste)   Charles Aznavour is the pianist who becomes involved in a Hollywood B-picture underworld plot and an impossible love affair with Marie Dubois with startling repercussions.
Subtitles   France 1960   Dir. Truffaut   Tuesday 7 pm

THE CRIME OF MONSIEUR LANGE (Le Crime de Monsieur Lange)   The film is a polemic against evil bosses and capitalist exploiters and for workers, solidarity and collectivism. Deep focus, mobile camera and improvised dialogue make it the first of Renoir's great 'realist' films.
Subtitles   France 1935   Dir. Renoir   Thursday 7 pm

Russian

BLUE MOUNTAINS (Golubye gory)   A satire set in a Soviet publishing house, behind whose walls work a devious group of editors and scribes, obsessed more with their own affairs, business meetings and lunches than with the fate of manuscripts left by aspiring authors.
Subtitles   USSR 1984   Dir. Eldar Shengelaya   Wednesday 7 pm

Word processing

(a)   Key in the note below, which is from you to Rebecca Andrews, who is taking over the running of the club, and print out one copy. Date it as today. No addresses are needed.

> Dear Rebecca
>
> As promised, I enclose some information about FCN which I hope will be of use to you. If anything is unclear please feel free to ring me at any time.
> I hope all goes well – good luck!
>
> Best wishes

(b)   Produce an amended version of 'FCN INFORMATION' (see below) and print out one copy.

FCN INFORMATION } *CENTRE*

Membership

Membership fees are as follows: *CHANGE # to £ SIGN*

Ordinary members	#59 per annum
Students	#35 per annum
Senior citizens	#5 per annum
Unwaged	#5 per annum

IN FULL Senior citizens, students and the unwaged must show their (id) cards when purchasing tickets. Membership fees can be paid in instalments by arrangement with the membership secretary.

Total membership, including this month's new members, is 796. The diagram below shows how this is made up.

INSERT CHART/GRAPH HERE   *JUSTIFY RIGHT MARGIN*

This month we have gained 15 new members, made up as indicated below.

INSERT CHART/GRAPH HERE

Choice of films

The annually elected committee selects films at ~~a~~ monthly
meeting, but all members are encouraged to put forward their
own suggestions to the committee. These can be made in
writing or by electronic mail on the viewdata system. Best
efforts will be made to obtain any films requested by
members.

Performances

~~If finances and other factors allow,~~ Six films are shown
per week. Performances usually start at 7.00 pm. Details
of the films are sent to members each month and can also be
accessed on the local viewdata system.

Disabled

There are ~~a~~ _three_ wheelchair positions at the rear of the
one auditorium and ~~a~~ specially adapted lavatory to the right of
the main entrance.

House rules

Standing during a performance is not permitted. Members
are asked to leave the building temporarily if they wish to
smoke.

Coffee bar

The coffee bar is open from ~~6.00~~ _5.30_ pm to 7.00 pm and serves
coffee, tea, juice and snacks. Alcohol is not served.

Collating the material

Attach the following to the note to Rebecca Andrews:

(1) The lists of new members from the database (the complete
one and the ones broken down into categories).

(2) An amended version of the FCN information sheet with the
two graphs/charts pasted in the appropriate position
(either electronically if possible, or manually, if not).

(3) Print-outs of the spreadsheet calculations.

(4) Print-outs of the viewdata pages, including routeing
information.

15   New Office Technology Exhibition

Word processing

(a)   Produce a word-processed copy of the standard letter to potential exhibitors about NOTE (New Office Technology Exhibition).

(b)   Produce a word-processed copy of Information for Exhibitors.

```
              Conference Organisers Inc
                    Brownmill
                     Watford
                      Herts
                Tel 0928 675531
```

Date today

Dear

An occasion to NOTE ...   } *bold - no underscore*

Following the resounding success of this year's NOTE (New
Office Technology Exhibition) we felt we should warn you
that if you wish to exhibit at next year's NOTE you need to
book a stand IMMEDIATELY.

We are taking even bigger premises for next year - the Town
Conference Centre - to accommodate more visitors and more
exhibitors. You can see from the chart below that for the
last few years the number of visitors to NOTE has been
rising dramatically and we expect this trend to continue.

insert chart/graph here

justify margin

This is an opportunity not to miss, if you sell any kind of
office technology product or service. Details of fees and
dates are attached. To book a stand fill in the form below
and return it now to avoid disappointment.

- 2 -

As well as the exhibition there will be talks going on during the day in the adjoining seminar rooms. If you wish to attend these talks, call Gillian Sanders on 0928 675531 to receive a programme and to book a place

Yours sincerely

Oliver Doe
Conference Organiser

Enc

NOTE

My company/organisation wishes to book a stand for NOTE on:

9 March ------ 10 March ------ 11 March ------ (tick days)

Name and address ---

Type of product/service ------------------------------------

size of stand   1 --------- 2 --------- (tick size)

extra lighting y/n -----   extra furniture set y/n -----

contact name ---

signature ------------------------------ date -------------

NEW   OFFICE TECHNOLOGY EXHIBITION (NOTE)

Information for Exhibitors

The exhibition will last three days, although exhibitors have the option to book a stand for just one or two days. However, it should be noted that preference will be given to those who opt for the full three days. If two days only are chosen, it must be two consecutive days.

There are two sizes of stands. Size 1 is: 6m x 4m and size 2 is: 8m x 6m. Those booking for more than one day must keep the same stand for the other day(s).

Fees are as follows:

	size 1 stand	size 2 stand
for one day	£500	£590
for two days	£750	£850
for three days	£900	£990

The following items are included in the price:
- A set of one desk + 2 chairs
- Lighting - one strip light + one spot light
- Two electricity points
- A name plate for above the stand
- Carpets

An additional furniture set of one desk + two chairs can be ordered at £45 per day.

Extra lighting - two spotlights - can also be ordered at £23 per day.

If you have any queries, please ring Gillian Sanderson on 0928 675531.

Graphics

The number of visitors to NOTE has been:

this year	3861
last year	2553
two years ago	1089
three years ago	902
four years ago	785

(a) Use an appropriate program to produce a bar chart/histogram to represent this information graphically. Use the correct year numbers, for example, 1988.

(b) Print out one copy of the chart.

Database

(a) Create a database file for the details of those who complete the forms to book a stand at NOTE. Use the following fields:

CONTACT
NAME
ADDRESS
TYPE

(b) Enter the details from the completed forms on page 93.

NEW OFFICE TECHNOLOGY EXHIBITION (NOTE)

My company/organisation wishes to book a stand for NOTE on:

9 March ...✓... 10 March ...✓... 11 March .....✓ (tick days)

Name and address *Technology Services Ltd, St Davids Hill, Brighton, Sussex*

Type of product/service *Hardware and software*

Size of stand 1 ..... 2 ...✓ (tick size)

Extra lighting (yes)/no ..... Extra furniture set (yes)/no .....

Contact name *Norman Midwinter*

Signature *N. Midwinter* Date ....

NEW OFFICE TECHNOLOGY EXHIBITION (NOTE)

My company/organisation wishes to book a stand for NOTE on:

9 March ..... 10 March ..... 11 March ...✓ (tick days)

Name and address *Training Specialists, 19 Pentel Rise, Glenrothes, Scotland*

Type of product/service *Training*

Size of stand 1 ...✓ 2 ..... (tick size)

Extra lighting yes/(no) ..... Extra furniture set yes/(no) .....

Contact name *Hugh Marsh*

Signature *H. Marsh* Date *7 March*

NEW OFFICE TECHNOLOGY EXHIBITION (NOTE)

My company/organisation wishes to book a stand for NOTE on:

9 March ...✓ 10 March ...✓ 11 March ..... (tick days)

Name and address *MIRROR SOFTWARE HOUSE, 15-19 WEST WAY, RICKMANSWORTH, HERTS*

Type of product/service *SOFTWARE + TRAINING*

Size of stand 1 ..✓ 2 ..... (tick size)

Extra lighting yes/(no) ..... Extra furniture set (yes)/no .....

Contact name *JAMES ALEXANDER*

Signature *James Alexander* Date ....

NEW OFFICE TECHNOLOGY EXHIBITION (NOTE)

My company/organisation wishes to book a stand for NOTE on:

9 March ...✓ 10 March ...✓ 11 March ...✓ (tick days)

Name and address *CONTEL COMPUTERS CONTEL HOUSE, LEAWAY ROAD, LIVERPOOL*

Type of product/service *HARDWARE + SOFTWARE*

Size of stand 1 ..... 2 ..✓ (tick size)

Extra lighting yes/(no) ..... Extra furniture set yes/(no) .....

Contact name *N. DOBSON (MR)*

Signature *N. Dobson* Date *1 December*

NEW OFFICE TECHNOLOGY EXHIBITION (NOTE)

My company/organisation wishes to book a stand for NOTE on:

9 March ...✓ 10 March ...✓ 11 March ...✓ (tick days)

Name and address *SOFTWARE SPECIAL, 11-15 MARKET WAY, EXETER, DEVON*

Type of product/service *SOFTWARE PACKAGES*

Size of stand 1 ...✓ 2 ..... (tick size)

Extra lighting yes/(no) ..... Extra furniture set (yes)/no .....

Contact name *J. BROWN (MS)*

Signature *J. Brown* Date *5/11*

For 'TYPE' use suitable abbreviations for the type of product or service that the company offers.

(c)   Print out one copy of all records with the company names in alphabetical order.

Videotex

A viewdata system will be available at NOTE with terminals in the conference centre, dining area, bar and seminar rooms for use by visitors and exhibitors.

(a)   Enter the details of the talks (as given below and opposite) on to a local viewdata system, routeing the pages as follows:

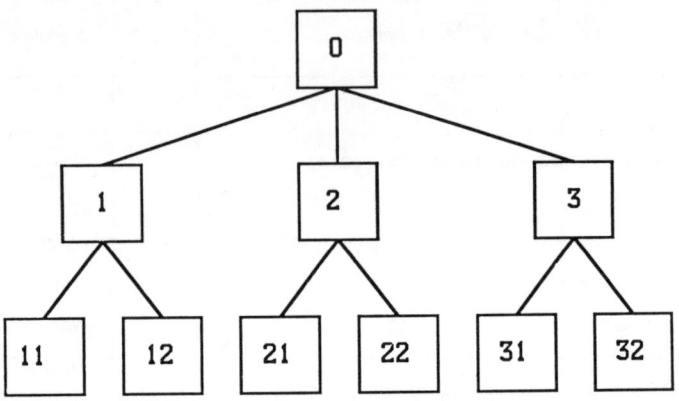

(b)   Print out the pages, including routeing information.

Page 0
1   9 March
2   10 March
3   11 March

Page 1
11   morning
12   afternoon

Page 2
21   morning
22   afternoon

Page 3
31   morning
32   afternoon

Page 11
"Will the office of the future by paperless" by Joyce Gregory of the Institute of Office Studies.

Page 12
''The changing role of the office worker'' by Jonathon Bright, author of ''Office Work 2000''.

Page 21
''Training for office skills'' by Dr Margaret Sentry, Principal of Wellington College of Further Education.

Page 22
''On-line databases—the state of the art'' by Chris Manning of Computer Services International.

Page 31
''Integrated Office Systems'' by Arthur Smith, Managing Director of The Office Automation Systems Group.

Page 32
''Artificial Intelligence in offices'' by Alexandra Coope, lecturer in AI and author of many works on the subject.

Spreadsheet

(a) Create a model which can be used to work out the invoices for each exhibitor based on:

- the number of days the stand is booked for
- the size of stand
- whether or not an extra furniture set and/or extra lighting is required

(b) Print out a copy of the model with the formulae.
(c) Use the model to calculate the fee for those who have already booked a stand (see completed forms).
(d) Print out copies of the calculations made in (c).

Collating the material

Collate the material in the following order:

(1) The standard letter with the tear-off form, incorporating the bar chart, pasted into the letter (either electronically, if possible, or manually, if not).
(2) The 'Information for Exhibitors' text.
(3) The print-out from the database file of the companies who have booked stands.
(4) Print-outs of the spreadsheet calculations.
(5) Print-outs of the viewdata pages, including routeing information.

16   Technical and Scientific Translation

Word processing

(a) Produce a word-processed version of the memo below and date it as today.

(b) Print out one copy.

(c) Produce a word-processed version of the text entitled 'Translation Rates', and print out one copy.

MEMO

To   B Keithly, Managing Director
From   A Fern, Marketing Manager

Date

Last year's sales figures

As requested, the figures for last year's sales:

(Insert graph/chart here)

I have arranged a meeting for next Monday at 3.00 pm to discuss the figures with the rest of my Department. I hope you, too, can attend. I have already asked Penny to put it in your diary.

TRANSLATION RATES } Centre

Notes for Marketing Staff

Figures below refer to rate per thousand words. The rates refer to 'normal' text i.e. sales material. For scientific text or for computer or car manuals, 5% is added. If a language is not listed here or if you are not sure about the nature of the text, discuss it with the Marketing Manager. Do not negotiate a discount for very large jobs without first discussing it with the Marketing Manager.

/justify

Language	To English	From English
	(pounds)	(pounds)
French	25	35
German	26	38
Italian	26	38
Spanish	30	40
Russian	42	50
Polish	40	48
Arabic	42	50
Swedish	40	50
Finnish	40	52
Norwegian	40	52
Hebrew	36	42
Chinese	45	55
Japanese	45	55
Gujarati	35	42
Farsi	40	50

put languages in alphabetical order

Graphics

Sales for last year were:

January	£5,526
February	£6,090
March	£12,349
April	£3,214
May	£8,675
June	£8,563
July	£4,002
August	£7,923
September	£10,814
October	£9,421
November	£9,165
December	£7,155

(a) Produce an appropriate graphical representation of the above information.

(b) Print out one copy.

Spreadsheet

(a) Create a spreadsheet model which can be used to calculate the cost to the customer of translating text.

The cost is dependent on:

(i) the number of words;
(ii) the language;
(iii) the content.

(b) Print out the model including the formulae.

(c) Look up the costs in the document created earlier entitled 'Translation Rates' and use the model to calculate the following:

(i) a car manual, 125,000 words, from English into German;

        (ii)   a sales brochure, 5,000 words, from English into Arabic;

        (iii) medical journals, 152,000 words, from Russian into English.

(d)   Print out the above calculations.

Database

(a)   Create a database file for details of freelance translators.

(b)   Choose suitable field names.

(c)   Enter the details of those translators listed below into the file.

(d)   Print out all records.

(e)   Search for translators suitable to do the three jobs outlined in (c) of the Spreadsheet section.

['General' means non-technical text. Assume translators can translate both to and from their language.]

(f)   Print out the records of those in (e).

Anna Schmidt, German, general
Christina Panatta, Italian, car manuals
Fernando Sanchez, Spanish, general
Hans Schneider, German, car manuals, computer manuals
Amtul Nuwas, Arabic, computer manuals, general
Yuri Zoshchenko, Russian, medicine, computer manuals
Ivan Rostov, Russian, geology, geography
Yong Ling, Chinese, general
M Svenson, Swedish, computer manuals, car manuals
Abu Hassan, Arabic, general
Claudio Esposito, Italian, car manuals
Sonya Markov, Russian, medicine
L Moghaddom, Farsi, general, computer manuals
Andreas Bergstrom, Swedish, medicine, computer manuals
A Bloom, Hebrew, general
J Kuczynska, Polish, general
Cecile Laurant, French, medicine, computer manuals
Hu Na, Chinese, medicine, geology
Joannes Axhausen, German, general, medical
B Paz, Spanish, computer manuals

Videotex

The Marketing, Translation and Production Departments of TEST each give a weekly 'update' on the local in-house viewdata system.

(a)   Routeing the pages appropriately, enter the details below.

(b)   Display the pages as effectively as possible.

(c)   Print out the pages, including routeing information.

Marketing

''There are three new jobs in the pipeline this week—a car manual, 125,000 words, from English into German, a sales brochure, 5,000 words, from English into Arabic and some medical journals, 152,000 words, from Russian into English. We're also bidding for a large job—manuals for the new Merrick van, which will mean translation into six languages. Several clients phoning about recent delays in production…Will be talking to production about that in detail!''

Translation

''We're still having problems finding Japanese translators, for technical work, particularly those able to translate INTO Japanese. Vice versa is OK. Other languages and subjects seem to be steady.''

Production

''With John and Moira still on holiday and Nigel leaving this month, we're still short-staffed so please don't offer clients unrealistic delivery dates. Check with us first. We're sure you'll all be pleased to know that we should actually finish the Council job this week!''

Collating the material

Collate the material in the following order:

(1) The memo, incorporating the graph for the sales figures, pasted in (electronically, if possible, or manually, if not).

(2) The 'Translation Rates' text.

(3)) Print-outs of the spreadsheet calculations.

(4) A print-out of all the database records and a print-out of those suitable for the three translation jobs referred to.

(5) Print-outs of the viewdata pages, including routeing information.

Index to Part I